Keep on Farmin'

Zen Ranching

and

The Farming Game

Zen Ranching

and

George Rohrbacher

BookPartners, Inc.
Wilsonville, Oregon

BookPartners, Inc.
P.O. Box 922
Wilsonville, Oregon 97070

To Ann with whom I fell in love at first sight, and to Betty who I grew to love through the passage of time.

Zen Ranching *n.* agricultural operations that take place primarily between the cars.

Table of Contents

1

Home on the Range

. . . .

"We'll take it," I said to Ann, as we stood peering in the broken window at the insects, by the hundreds, swarming the walls and windows inside the vacant cottage. A tattered screen fluttered in the breeze around the jagged hole in the windowpane. A flying beer bottle had ripped through the screen and glass and lay on the dusty floor of the empty living room in the small one-story shanty.

Ann, as anxious as I to find a house we could call home, said cheerfully, "It'll take some work."

The house was located six miles from Toppenish, Washington, a genuine Western town complete with cowboys and dirty pickup trucks. We learned later that the house was situated at a place the locals called Three Bridges. The infrequently traveled road to Three Bridges, judging by the dusty cans and bottles that winked in the roadside weeds, was evidently motor party heaven. As for the little white house, it desperately needed a new coat of paint on the outside. The inside wasn't too bad, except for the bugs and broken glass, since the walls had been given a fairly recent cosmetic renewal with paint. The facelift was enough to make the plain, four-room cabin look like heaven to us. It was to be our first real home as newlyweds.

The environment we chose for our first home was dramatically different from the ones Ann and I had grown up in. My dad had been a research biochemist, and we had lived in the suburbs of Eastern university towns. But during my last two years at college in Denver, where I met Ann, I lost my heart to her and to America's wilderness in the high mountains of Colorado.

I would have been stupid and blind not to understand her parents' initial opposition to our marriage. I was a bearded, unemployed college student, lacking any material assets. Out of the blue I had captured the heart of their daughter who had been involved for a year with a young man whose social and economic standing was beyond question. Ann's family was affluent; her father was the CEO of a bank in Seattle. Ann's parents disapproved of me instantly and opposed our marriage.

But with Ann and I, it was love at first sight. We saw each other for the first time on a Tuesday. We talked to one another for the first time on Wednesday; I walked her to class on Thursday; and then we flew to Seattle to meet her family on Friday. A week later I asked Ann to marry me. Without hesitation she said yes. With the grudging approval of her parents, we married in June.

Ann and I agreed that I would defer graduate school in anthropology for a year, so that we could see America before we became enslaved to careers, mortgages, insurance payments, or dirty diapers. At the end of that ten month trip of discovery, covering thirty-seven states, we were convinced that we wanted to try life in rural America first hand. The cabin at Three Bridges was our opportunity.

I think that my yearning for the open spaces was the result of being raised in a housing development among the potato and barley fields of New Jersey, near the Princeton Junction train station. Every morning, five days a week, suburban-dwelling executives parked their cars for the forty-mile commuter train ride into their office buildings among the skyscrapers of New York City. At night, they arrived back home clutching their *Wall Street Journals* with worn looks on their faces. I wanted something different, less constricting.

Ann, a Western girl by birth, loved the outdoors, and as a child growing up in Seattle went skiing, camping, or horseback riding at every opportunity. We both had aspirations of waking to the sounds of birds in the air and wind in the trees. We dreamt of living in a place where the night sky filled to overflowing with blazing starlight. It was a dream we knew was only possible if we lived in the country.

Optimists that we were, all the while we searched for a place to settle down, we avoided the question of how we would support ourselves once we landed. Being young, vigorous and impractical, we concluded that we were smart enough to sketch in the details when we got there.

Ann and I felt lucky to find the little white cottage near Toppenish. It was part of a deal that made us caretakers for a duck-hunting club. We were to do maintenance chores, and for our labor we would earn the princely sum of $1.90 an hour applied to the rent for our little four-room house.

It wasn't until a week later, on Memorial Day weekend, when Ann and I arrived with the first of our two pickup loads of housewares, that we actually realized we were moving into a mosquito-infested swamp. That was the same weekend when a record heat wave settled into the Yakima Valley and all of Eastern Washington.

Three Bridges, where we took up housekeeping, was located at the southern end of the Yakima Valley, an area famous for apples, pears, hops, wine grapes, and a long growing season. While it is high desert, it is well-irrigated and surrounded by mountains and bisected by a river. Dominating the valley are the distant, snow-clad glaciers on Mount Adams and Mount Rainier.

Regardless of the Yakima Valley's reputation as one of the premier apple-growing regions in the world, there were no fruit trees of any kind within sight of the duck-hunting club. In fact, with the exception of a tangle of willow brush along the banks of Toppenish Creek and a lone poplar tree in our backyard, the view from our cabin was unobstructed. Ann and I could see for miles in most directions across an expanse of sagebrush and bunchgrass. We were smack in the middle of cattle country, with real cows complete with honest-to-goodness cowboys and Indians.

Soon after we finished transferring the first load of our belongings from our truck into the barren little cabin, Ann suggested that we take a drive look-see across Toppenish Creek. We needed to explore what was on the other side of the wall of willows. We had two fairly close neighbors on our side of the creek: one, half a mile to the west; and the other, three-quarters of a mile to the north, but we had no idea of who might live on the other side.

The county road, after crossing the first of the three bridges for which our area was named, wound through a tangle of underbrush and chest-high, canary reedgrass islands that teemed with insect life and the birds feeding on it. The landscape past the third and final bridge was pancake flat, sagebrush and grasses running to the horizon both east

Cow Country

and west. Straight ahead to the south, about a mile away, Toppenish Ridge towered above the surrounding openness.

On the bank of the creek beside the last bridge sat a large, windowless, two-story Victorian house. It had been grand in its day, but judging from its sun-bleached wooden siding and gaping cedar shingles, that day had been long ago. Howie Wright, the duck club owner, said that the Victorian had been an old stage stop. We could easily imagine a freshly watered team of horses and coach pulling out for the trip over the ridge to Goldendale, some fifty miles away.

On the opposite side of the road from the defunct stage stop was an irrigated pasture of sixty acres, punctuated by a small, lonely, red clapboard house whose front doorstep practically rested on the shoulder of the county road.

"I bet they don't miss a thing that goes by," Ann joked. As if on cue, as we passed the red house, a curtain pulled back and unseen eyes inspected us. Beyond the tiny outpost, there were no more dwellings — nothing but sagebrush and saltgrass in alkali patches surrounded by mats of thick fescue grasses thriving in the sub-irrigated low spots.

As we drove along the county road we noticed fresh evidence that Three Bridges was cattle country. Cow tracks were visible in the gravel, and the still-juicy cow pies meant they had been deposited by critters who had recently passed this way. A hawk spooked from a power pole as we drove by circled off to the west towards Mount Adams. At the foot of Toppenish Ridge, we turned around and headed back along the way we'd come, this time noticing the signs — National Wildlife Refuge — that hung from the fenceposts on the east side of the road all the way back to the old stage stop. It struck me then that the obvious plan of the duck club next door to the refuge was to pick off all the ducks who were too dumb to read.

We recrossed Three Bridges, past our new home, and continued the six miles into town to buy some window putty, a new piece of glass, and a few cans of Raid. Toppenish, we discovered, was the headquarters of the Confederated Tribes of the Yakama Indian Nation. The duck club was on deeded land within the reservation. In the shimmering heat Toppenish was every inch a cowboy town, where every third vehicle was a pickup truck, and Toppenish's inhabitants seemed to be mainly men who wore straw hats with a weave that allowed for ventilation.

We drove past Logan's Feed and Seed, standing on one corner at the main town crossroads facing an old movie house on one side and a drugstore on the other. The June sun blazed down with an intensity that Ann and I weren't accustomed to, and my lily-white forearm, hanging out the window of the truck door in the noonday sun, was growing pink from exposure. The bank thermometer read ninety-six degrees.

There was plenty of parking in front of the building supply store. We pulled up next to a battered flatbed truck carrying enough road dust to grow a crop of potatoes. Waves of heat wiggled across the blacktop. The sun glinting off a stack of brand-new thirty-gallon galvanized garbage cans; made my eyes water from their reflection.

A few hours later, back at our house with the window repaired and our gear unpacked, I lay exhausted, neck deep in a bathtub full of cold water, trying to evade the omnipresent heat. A newfound feeling of self-reliance crept over me as I thought of the gassed mosquitoes and flies that buzzed and spun on their backs in all corners of the house as they succumbed to the vapors from the insect bomb.

Having spent my whole life, except for a couple summer jobs, behind a desk, I wanted a change. I desperately wanted to learn to work with my hands, to produce some tangible product at the end of the day, not just to be some loop on an office paper trail.

The next morning as dawn was breaking, we left Three Bridges for the long drive to Seattle to get our last load of belongings: some secondhand furniture, a stereo, and a stack of wedding presents that had been in storage for a year while we had been off seeing America. Once in the city, we hurriedly loaded our pickup and returned to Toppenish late the same day. Ann and I were finally housekeeping on our own. We were as giddy as newlyweds, though we'd been married almost a full year.

As we pulled into our fenced yard, after the three-and-a-half-hour drive from Seattle, it seemed that the little white cabin had shrunk in our absence. The sun was hot and the wind blowing ten to fifteen miles per hour from the west. There was just enough air moving to keep the mosquitoes down hiding in the grass. Ann and I started unloading the truck. We had a long list of things to get done before dark. While we unpacked, we joked with each other that we no longer would put our worldly possessions in a backpack to head off to see faraway places. We were finished with traveling. We were getting settled. We were raring to buckle down and get to work.

As I headed out the door to get another armload of household goods, a car slowly pulled into the driveway. The gravel barely made a sound under the balding tires of the '56 Oldsmobile. By the look of the sedan's paint job, it had been driven through the brush more than once. I recognized it as the vehicle which had been parked in front of the neighbor's red house across the creek.

Smiling in anticipation, I said to Ann, "Here we are barely moved in and we've got our very first visit from any of our neighbors, our first dose of good old country hospitality."

Anxious to make the acquaintance of our visitors, I walked over to the car. The passenger side window rolled down, revealing a weathered and rusty-looking old man. He had week-old stubble on his face and down his leathery neck. A cigarette dangled from his near-toothless mouth and dropped ashes on his filthy, grease-stained workshirt. Next to him, behind the steering wheel, sat a large Indian woman in a cotton day dress, with a Little Orphan Annie hairdo and rhinestone-studded glasses. The man waved a gnarled and dirty finger in my face. Then, in a blast of whiskey-soaked breath, he demanded, "Just who and how many of you is moving in here?"

I stood in stunned silence for a moment, and then before he could repeat his question, I answered, "Just my wife and me."

He squinted his red eyes at me as if to answer, then he spat a stream of tobacco juice onto the driveway. He turned and mumbled something to the woman at the wheel, who then backed the car out on the road, and they headed across the creek for home.

If this was the welcoming committee, I guessed we weren't likely to be invited to taffy pulls or quilting bees at the local grange hall anytime too soon.

2

Didn't Everybody Want to Grow Up to be a Cowboy?

• • • • • • • • • • • • • • •

The Yakima Valley's record-breaking heat wave continued to build day after day, until even the nights were no longer cool; the only relief came during the wee hours of the morning. June and July saw thirty-eight straight days above ninety degrees, with fifteen of those days in the hundreds. The canary reedgrass in the pasture surrounding our house sucked up all the swamp water and by the Fourth of July was fifteen feet tall and thick enough to hide an elephant and ten million insects along with it.

Ann and I had toiled like slaves to make a garden spot out of a small plot next to the cabin. It had apparently been used, in years previous, for extra parking. We planned to raise a dozen different vegetables to feed ourselves as much as possible and can the extra to fill our pantry. The dirt was hard as a brick and covered with a dense sod. We broke the soil out inch by inch in the traditional low-tech manner — with a shovel. In our little barnyard there was no shortage of composted manure, so we added plenty of it to the newly turned dirt and planted our first garden.

Above our heads, as we worked in the dirt, hovered a dense cloud of 'skeeters. The clouds were so thick that we had to wear protective clothing and a liberal coating of Off. Sucking a mosquito down the windpipe was as much a likelihood in our vegetable patch as blisters.

Almost immediately, Ann got a job as a bank teller in the neighboring town of Union Gap. She majored in math in college, had summer teller work experience, and banking was in her blood, since her dad and granddad were bankers. She left the university after her junior year to marry me before finishing her degree. We both agreed that her job would only be temporary, until both of us went back to school the following year.

Union Gap, a suburb of the city of Yakima, boasted an interesting history. Union Gap was the original site of the city of Yakima until 1895 when the Northern Pacific Railway Company convinced the whole town to move lock, stock and hitching post five miles north to a different site that the railroad was promoting. The site surrounded the newly constructed rail and switching yard. After the wholesale defection of her town folk, Yakima became known as Union Gap. It had taken nearly a century for the city of Yakima to grow large enough to cover the distance back to the original location and the few diehards that stayed behind.

At the duck club I had several months of work ahead of me, doing every possible kind of repair. Howie Wright, the owner, who recently purchased the place, presented me with a long list of improvement projects. Howie was the Northwest's construction king. Among other ventures, he was builder and part owner of the Seattle Space Needle. He bought the duck club as a getaway, a place to entertain in a rustic fashion. The club consisted of the main house and our caretaker's cabin, eighty acres of open fields, and two large shallow ponds between the meanders of Toppenish Creek. The duck blinds were built into the rose bushes that grew chest high on the earthen berms along the edges of the ponds, which were flooded only in the fall for hunting. Toppenish Creek, on the south edge of the club, was outlined with willow brush. The cover made for excellent jump shooting of pheasant and quail, as well as ducks.

I was fully aware that work at the duck club was to be only part time after the first major projects were completed. One or two days a week I rode the twenty-five miles into Yakima with Ann on her way to work in our only vehicle, looking for a full-time job of my own. Two months later I was still without one, but I developed the beginnings of a worry-induced ulcer. Rescue came in the form of the Federal Emergency Employment Act of 1971. School districts were the main beneficiary of the federal funding, and I, minus my beard and long hair, ended up late October as a teacher's aide at Wilson Junior High School.

The daily fifty-mile round trip from Three Bridges to Yakima and Union Gap was eating up our half-ton pickup truck right before our eyes. Ann and I decided that we had to buy a commuter car soon if we wanted our pickup to survive. The $2,600, twenty-four-month auto loan we took out to buy a VW bug felt as formidable to us as the national debt. The loan payments attached themselves like leeches to our skimpy paychecks. The bank where Ann worked had strict rules about overdrafts and missed payments by their employees. From the beginning she was determined to pay off the car loan early, and to achieve that goal, I was forbidden to carry more than $5 and allowed only enough bank checks to cover the shopping stops on my list. Ann took complete charge of our checkbook, and she squeezed and squeezed our budget until we were making nearly double payments on the car loan, hoping to clear it out in eighteen months or less.

Fall turned to winter, and ducks poured into the valley in huge quacking wedges. The shooting at Howie's duck club was fabulous. Unfortunately for Howie, he was so busy with business that he was able to hunt on only three weekends all season. It fell to me to take up the slack. Part of my job as duck club caretaker was to patrol for poachers. I took my job seriously. Weekday mornings before school, I put three shells in my shotgun and made my rounds. The jump shooting on Toppenish Creek was usually so good that I almost always came home with one or two ducks for my efforts. Ann and I were literally living off the land, eating a steady diet of mallards and canned vegetables from our garden. We soon ate enough duck in every conceivable form to last us a lifetime.

Darcella, our nearest neighbor, a quarter of a mile up the creek, was the recent bride of a cowboy known as Jim. She was Jim's second wife. Though not quite twenty, she had just become the mother of Jim's two teenage kids, Roger and Anita Fay. They made life hell for Darcella, and she did her best to return the favor. Jim was like thousands of other modern cowboys. He worked at a factory Monday through Friday, and on weekends he roped steers and chased somebody else's cows. Jim wore glasses and was never seen in public without his cowboy hat. He was in his forties and was developing significant trophy belt buckle overhang.

From our first week on Toppenish Creek, Ann bought fresh milk and eggs from Jim and Darcella, and almost immediately they started treating her like family. Along with the milk, Ann came home day after day with new hilarious stories of the goings-on next door. Over coffee, in their sparsely furnished kitchen, there seemed to be no subject too private for Darcella to discuss, from her mother-in-law's bladder operation, to family finance, to who was sleeping with whom in the neighborhood. No matter the nature of the domestic catastrophe, Ann found Darcella wound up each morning waiting to have someone to share it with. Jim and Darcella's approach to the twists and turns of life was humor.

Jim was a heeler in team-roping contests held all over the Northwest. Like many in the fraternity of ropers, the first knuckle of his left thumb was missing. It had been pruned off in a rope dally around the saddlehorn when a big steer hit the end of the loop, squeezing off his thumb. The accident happened before reattachment surgery was common, and Jim's blue heeler dog, Tailgate, found the severed digit in the corral dirt and gulped it down, as the attendants applied first aid with Jack Daniels and a clean handkerchief.

Jim lived for his weekends. Loading up his horse and heading off to a jackpot roping or small-town rodeo formed the purpose and rhythm of Jim's life. His pay stubs might have said factory worker, but in his heart he was 100 percent cowboy. He couldn't help it if the pioneering era to which he truly belonged had passed. He was a plain-spoken old cowpoke and a little wall-eyed on account of a corral board which collided with his face years before while he was breaking a colt. Though well into middle age, Jim could still throw a rope good enough to take the prize money on occasion, and small prizes like these were just enough to keep him at it.

"You're looking at one hell of a piece of manpower, son," Jim said, as he peglegged his way across the wintery barnyard towards me. He was covered from head to foot with the blood and slime of a newborn calf. "Damn big calf; practically had to pull it in two to get it out. Huge; we're going to have to use a different bull on our milk cow the next time. Damn! Honey," he waved at Darcella, "get me a beer. Say, get one for the neighbor, too."

"I don't drink beer so soon after breakfast; it plays hell with my Cheerios," I said, declining the offer and checking my watch to see it was nine o'clock.

"Hell, I just got off graveyard shift a few hours ago," Jim said. "It's suppertime for me. Here I come home to find Darcella's milk cow in labor, everything ass backwards and upside down. I'd never seen such a damn mess," Jim said, wiping his hands on his soiled home-sewn, pearl-buttoned, floral print cowboy shirt. The quickly drying mucus from the new calf that covered his hands had picked up dozens of little pieces of straw and manure, and blood had found the deep and gnarled cracks and crevices of his skin. Jim's hands had seen some hard use, and when covered with the birth goo they looked a thousand years old.

Darcella came out of the house with Jim's beer and a Pepsi for herself. Her youthful, curvaceous body was barely hidden beneath Jim's flowing, rough flannel shirt.

"Hey, why can't I have a Pepsi?" whined Anita Fay, as she ventured onto the porch.

Darcella whirled around, her golden hair splaying out like a cat with its back up. "I told you to finish up that washing, and I mean now!" she hissed.

The screen door slammed as Anita Fay retreated back into the house. Her haste spoke of many previous battles, none of which she'd won. Darcella then turned, as pretty as you please, and walked over and handed her husband his beer. Jim downed half of it in one swig.

"Well, you big dummy, did you save the calf or not?" Darcella asked.

Jim looked long and hard at his boots and answered with a poker face, "Hell yes, but I don't think the calf knows it yet. Roger is still in the barn with the cow. We're going to have to milk her out and put some of that first milk down the calf." He paused as a smile crept over his lips. "That poor little sucker won't make it if'n he don't get some of that colostrum milk right away. That applies to any calf, and to one who came into this world as hard as this one, it applies double."

Jim took another swig, almost draining the beer bottle. He cocked his head in the direction of the barn and said to me, "Well, you want to come and look at the little fart?"

"Sure," I said, and we headed over to the barn. Jim's walk suggested that his major parts were not all lined up exactly. Whether it was his past days of glory at the rodeo or his honky-tonkin' nights, he had put one heck of a lot of wear and tear on the equipment.

"Jim, honey, did that cow kick you? You're walking all stove up," Darcella asked in a mocking sort of way.

"Why, Darcella, you knowed there was mileage on me before we got married," Jim said with a broad, sugar-sweet smile.

"Yeah, but I didn't count on your transmission being out!" she barked back.

"Honey, now..." Jim said, in his chicken-fried country twang.

Just then, the old cow tried to stagger to her feet, her hind legs still wobbly from the difficult birth. Jim vaulted over the fence to prevent the cow from stomping her helpless newborn, and to escape the next jab from Darcella's sharp tongue.

Jim took a calf bottle and milked one of the cow's teats until the container was half full. The calf fought Jim with all its strength to keep from being bottle fed, but after Jim got a big slug of fresh milk down him, the calf stopped fighting and started sucking for all he was worth. The little fellow quickly drained the remains of the bottle. Charlotte the cow settled down as Jim milked the rest of the front quarter into the calf bottle for a later feeding.

"Roger," Jim shouted at his son, "you go on into the house and get the bucket! Charlotte has to be milked all around before she splits a tit," Jim ordered. "Then come back and finish milking her out. As much as she's got; this calf could never use it all. Feed the colostrum milk to the pigs, but save some for Tailgate." He looked at me and said, "Let's go on in and wash up; I'm ready for another beer."

Jim and Darcella's house was very much like our own, only without the benefit of a remodel. The west wind was picking up, and the tin roof over the porch rattled as the screen door slammed behind us. The January morning had started out brisk and frosty with over a half a foot of snow on the ground, but with the wind blowing the temperature was rapidly warming. It felt like spring. The thermometer on the porch within an hour climbed from below freezing to fifty-four degrees.

"Hooooweee, are we ever having a Chinook!" exclaimed Jim, opening up yet another beer. The curtains inside the house danced on the breeze coming through the clapboard walls. The barnyard filled with the sound of dripping as the past two weeks' snow started to melt off the metal roofs of the barn and ragged outbuildings. Jim looked lazily out the window and predicted that if the Chinook wind didn't quit soon, it would start flooding by dinner. His prediction didn't miss by much.

About midnight Toppenish Creek left her banks. The surrounding land was tabletop flat for several miles on either side of the creek, and by morning our place, the duck club, and the wildlife refuge next door were covered by a vast sheet of water. The warming Chinook wind kept up through the night, and in the morning not a trace of snow could be seen on the neighboring low-lying hills. Only the high country in the Cascades still held snow. Mount Adams, white and silent in the distance, stood out on the skyline framed in the bright blue, freshly washed winter sky. On Jim's advice, we had moved our vehicles over to the main house of the duck club, which stood several feet higher than the rest of the surrounding territory. It was good advice; the county road, from our house at Three Bridges to past Jim and Darcella's driveway, was soon under two feet of water. Jim assured me that in the three years he'd rented his place on the creek he had never known the water to get so high as to flood either of our houses. He was right again; the flood waters peaked at the top step of our back porch.

The second night, after the warm Pacific storm had blown itself out, the mercury started to drop again. After the shot of fifty-five-degree weather, it was hard to believe that it was still early January, but by the time the thermometer hit zero the following evening, I was reassured. The cold weather staunched the floods, and soon the county road reappeared enough for us to be able to hang up our hip waders and start driving all the way home again.

Jim had relocated his vehicles to the main house of the duck club at the start of the flood. He had also moved his four horses and milk cow to a paddock beside the main house. The new baby calf couldn't make the trip because the quick change in the weather had killed him. Jim explained that the previous duck club owner had allowed him to use the paddock as an emergency flood procedure.

I agreed.

After a week of near-zero temperatures the countryside surrounding our house became one vast skating rink. By crossing a few half-submerged fences, Ann and I could ice skate for miles across the covered fields. The skating lasted until the next Chinook wind three weeks later. The winter brought two more warm winds and more high water. Walking home a third of a mile in hip waders with an armload of groceries soon ceased to be an adventure and became one royal pain. The floodwater in the fields didn't subside until May, and by that time Jim's livestock had turned Howie's paddock into a mess. The horses had almost eaten the grass right down to the dirt by the time Jim moved them home.

Howie's secretary called and said the boss could be expected over Memorial Day weekend. She wanted me to make sure the place was ready for inspection. After a few days of warm Yakima Valley spring weather and some water, the pasture recovered to look almost as good as new. Nature soon covered all evidence of my unauthorized executive decision.

About this same time, my year at Wilson Junior High reached its low point. I had taken over an art class the last period of the day, riding herd over a rambunctious seventh-grade crew who drove their teacher, a fifty-two-year-old divorcée, to the point of a mental breakdown. For most of the spring term she had sat mute in her corner, shellshocked, barely surviving another day to the eighth period. She watched appreciatively while I took up the whip and chair to defend her against the little monsters.

One warm and beautiful afternoon the next-to-last week of school, Julie, the sassiest little monster in the bunch, intentionally spilled her bottle of india ink and ruined the work of everyone who was unfortunate enough to sit at her table.

"Hormones," we had all said in the teacher's lounge; Julie just had a double dose. This minor catastrophe sent my older colleague shrieking down the hall in the direction of the office.

"Julie," I said when I confronted her, "after you clean up the mess, stay seated when the rest of the class is dismissed. You're going to spend half an hour in detention after school today."

The rest of the class snickered but quickly clammed up when I shot a fiery glance over their faces, a warning of how easily they might join her. Tending to several truant children was no harder than just one, and they knew it. The class settled down and was soon dismissed.

As Julie was attacking the chewing gum stalactites under her table with a putty knife, about ten minutes into her sentence my classroom door came flying open with a bang!

It was Julie's mother! She was steaming mad! In the most foul and abusive language possible, she told me that she had been waiting for her little darling out in the parking lot with the motor running. Fifteen goddamn minutes late for her hairdresser's appointment. (Her further expletives are deleted.) She wanted her daughter immediately!

I told her firmly that Julie would have to remain at her task and if she wished to discuss the problem further she should please take it up with the principal, who could be found in his office at the other end of the building. My answer unleashed another floodgate of obscenities. Had her tirade come from a man, I probably would have taken a punch at him. But as it was, I stood as calm and possessed as possible and let her verbal abuse flow over me without visible effect. At that moment, I made two decisions: Julie was going to serve her full term of gum scraping no matter what her foul-mouthed mother said, and I definitely wasn't going to be coming back in the fall for another round of junior high.

I decided to take a job driving tractor, offered to me by one of the neighbors, a Yakama Indian rancher named Swede Carl. It seemed a good opportunity to check out farming firsthand, learn the ropes, and get paid to boot.

I thought Swede was a funny name for an Indian, but apparently he liked it better than his given name, Delbert. There was nothing funny about the way he ran a ranch, though; Swede was all business, twelve hours a day, six days a week and Sundays too, if it was harvest time. He rose at four a.m., four-thirty in the winter. While planning the day's operations, he drank about a pot and a half of coffee and chewed on his pipe stem until the hired man arrived for work at six-forty-five a.m. As my tires crunched on the gravel pulling into the yard, Swede would practically kick the screen door off its hinges, as he flew outside under a caffeine-powered head of steam.

Over the din of barking stock dogs, he shouted the orders while walking from the house in my direction. After getting lined out, we talked for a few minutes until seven a.m. sharp, and then I started work. There was never a slack moment until lunch, which I ate at the house with Swede and his family. Liz, Swede's wife, was an iron-willed mistress of her kitchen, and tolerated no procrastination at mealtimes. I was happy to be cleaned up and waiting on the dot of twelve o'clock, never late, because of meals like her red eye gravy and chicken-fried steak.

On my first day of work at Swede's, I was to start planting a twenty-acre field to alfalfa. I had never driven a tractor before, but Swede was willing to spend the extra time it took to break in a green hand. His lessons on operating the cantankerous International Model M tractor ended with the admonishment that if I made any skips while I was seeding the stand of alfalfa, they would be visible for a decade. He also said if I turned too short, ran the tractor wheel up on the hitch of the seed drill and broke anything, I would be fired. With that, he left to go check on some cows up in the mountains.

Luckily, I turned out to be a natural-born equipment operator, and Swede soon turned all the hay swathing, baling and stacking with the self-propelled bale wagon over to me. I learned to irrigate and fix fence. I learned to become a mechanic on the equipment I was operating. I wasn't afraid to show my ignorance and ask questions. And Swede wasn't a bit shy about telling me how to do anything, even if I hadn't asked. The better I got at running the ranch down in the valley, the more time Swede spent checking cows in the mountains.

Swede and his summer range partner, Glen, ran their cows together on more than 60,000 acres. The range reached from the valley grass and sagebrush up to the high country's tamarack and fir timber. The Yakama Tribe had many members who were exceptionally able stockmen, going back to Chief Kamiakin, their great leader in the 1870s.

Swede was a great teacher, and I learned how to cowboy from him, chasing his and Glen's cows across the hills and canyons of the reservation. Before moving to the valley I had never ridden a horse, not even the pony ride at the county fair. My family were not farmers, not for a few generations. My dad's first job was with the USDA, as a research scientist, when we lived in Auburn, Alabama. That was as close to farm life as we had ever gotten. Ann, on the other hand, had been a regular *National Velvet* as a child. She had ridden horses from a young age and had read *Black Beauty* next to a warming fireplace, waiting out Seattle's winter rain. Ann loved to ride and had gotten me started too, almost as soon as we settled in at Three Bridges.

To save expenses, most of our neighbors trailed their cattle, whenever possible, instead of hauling them by truck. Many times throughout the year, cows had to be moved to new pastures; so there was always an opportunity to sharpen one's cowpunching skills. Most cattlemen had a few friends from town willing to give up their weekends to go punch cows for free. As the greenest of greenhorns, I was happy as could be, riding any spare horse that could be found. I loved a cattle drive. The first time I got behind a herd of slow-moving cows trailing across the hills, my mind flashed back to the traffic jams in New Jersey at Princeton Circle on Route 1, during rush hour. Then, with the squeak of saddle leather under my seat and amid trail dust, a feeling of peace and well-being I had never known before settled over me.

That year, while we were moving cows on Glen and Swede's range, I learned a lot about a beef cow's mothering instincts and her indelible memory for country, for where the salt and water and best feed are located. During the annual turnout in early April, I had seen a fine example of how well a cow can remember the territory. We had driven Glen's cows and baby calves about fifteen miles the first day, over Toppenish Ridge, to the corrals at the old lambing camp up on Logy Creek. We penned the herd of a couple hundred Herefords for the night, and then moved them twelve miles higher into the canyon lands, where we turned them loose into their 1,500-acre breeding pasture.

The following morning, down in the valley we found one of those cows at Glen's front gate. She'd traveled through three or four fences and returned all the way home, twenty-five miles in the dark, bawling for her calf. Glen opened the gate to the quarter section of sagebrush, where the whole herd had spent the night before the cattle drive began two days earlier. Bellowing and slobbering, frantic with worry, the cow made a beeline through the brush to the gully that cut through the back of the place. There, under a greasewood bush, she found her baby. The calf, somehow missed by the riders, had stayed put just where its mother had left it forty-eight hours earlier. This mothering ability is the trait that's the backbone of the range cow business.

Late one day we had moved all the cows to summer range, and were headed back to the stock truck. Glen, Swede and I rode three abreast down a power line road that cut across the grass-covered hills to service a high-tension line carrying electricity from the Hanford Nuclear Reservation to the BPA grid at the Bonneville Dam on the Columbia River. All four of the stock dogs tagged behind us with their tongues hanging out. They had put on at least thirty miles since morning running after the cows, up and down the hills on the six-hour ride.

Riding Dingbat — a little black horse that pranced constantly — had rubbed my behind nearly raw. When the access road crested the last rise and we finally saw Swede's stock truck about a mile and a half away, I made a decision. If Dingbat still wanted his head, after carrying me up and down those canyons all day long, he could have it. I slacked off the tension on the reins and Dingbat took off like a rocket. It was as if he, too, saw the truck. Glen and Swede picked up their pace, and in ten strides we were in a horse race.

Swede was riding a chestnut quarterhorse that quickly left us in the dust. Glen wasn't pushing his young bay gelding, who looked nearly as pooped as the dogs. After about the first hundred yards, Glen and Swede dropped back, leaving Dingbat the only contestant in this race. It was fine with me if my horse wanted to run; the pain of my saddle-sore butt would just be over that much sooner. About a half-mile from the truck I started to pull back on the reins, lest Dingbat forget I was still up there. I was soon pulling with all my strength, and Dingbat was not responding; his short neck was like a steel rod that gave a little, but would not bend. At one-quarter mile and closing on the truck, I was pulling with everything I had.

I had played defensive tackle in high school, was in reasonably good shape and not intimidated by my pint-sized runaway. Again, I yanked with all my might on the reins. The chain under Dingbat's chin parted and his hackamore bridle became as useless as a pair of earrings.

"Holy shit!" was the only thought that crossed my mind.

The five-wire gate was shut across the road between us and the truck. When Dingbat finally saw the gate, it was only ten yards away and far too late to stop. I was sitting very loose in the saddle going over my options, none of them good, when Dingbat hit the gate going nearly full throttle. POP! The gate sticks snapped, the wire broke. I was airborne. Twenty feet later, I hit the ground hard after doing a half-gainer. Stunned, I watched Dingbat rise from his knees and shake off the remains of the barbed-wire gate and the saddle rigging. Then he walked over and loaded himself into the truck.

When I slowly stood up, demonstrating that I wasn't hurt, Glen and Swede burst out laughing. With the remains of half a bottle of whiskey, conveniently hidden under a rock near the destroyed gate, we nursed my wounded pride. Glen laughed until he cried.

3

Digging In

- - - - - - - - - - - - - - - - - - - -

By the end of our second summer at Three Bridges, Ann and I had decided we wanted to make Eastern Washington our home. The dry climate was ideal. There were four very distinct seasons that included everything from an occasional subzero blizzard to desert heat capable of cooking lunch on the sidewalk. Our second summer in the valley was mild, a welcome change from the first, which had been broiling. The temperature reached into the nineties only three days, and never once broke the one hundred mark.

Our ranching neighbors, with few exceptions, were friendly and more than willing to help fill in the blanks in our rural educations. Many of our older neighbors, with sixth-grade educations and Ph.D.s in practical experience, gladly took on a college boy for a student. Nobody ever locked their house and always left the keys in the ignition of the pickup truck out front without fearing it would be stolen. The valley was a good place to live.

The agricultural bounty and diversity that seemed to pour forth from the rich soils of the valley also captivated my imagination. Yakima County produced an incredible thirty different crops, grossing millions of dollars annually. Such productivity was infectious, and during our first summer Ann and I made a small start at farming. We borrowed $1,200 from the bank and bought a milk cow, a yearling heifer, two feeder steers, and eight calves to run on the canary reedgrass pasture that came with our caretaker's house. The four steer calves and four heifer calves were not weaned, so we raised them on a bottle supplemented with grain.

Later, after they had grown some, we turned the calves out with the others. Ten months later, the sale of the steers paid the total expenses on the whole project. At the end of our first year's farming venture, we owned five heifers and a milk cow free and clear. Our barnyard menagerie grew to include dogs, cats, chickens, and horses of our own. Everyday life in the country agreed with us more and more!

As another fall term passed, Ann and I made the decision to put my graduate school plans on hold indefinitely, and to stay in the valley. We decided it was time to try again to find a place of our own, a small fruit ranch somewhere off the Yakama Reservation. I decided that the complications of non-Indians owning land within the reservation was something I didn't want to deal with. We decided to concentrate our search for property across the Yakima River, in the fruit districts of Zillah, Outlook and Sunnyside.

We were looking for a ten- or twenty-acre farm, with good land and an older but still livable house. We hoped to find a parcel with a few acres in a high-value crop like orchard, and some open land for our growing herd of cattle. In January I found a ratty little dump of a house on twenty-seven acres of Class A soil, including five acres of concord grapes. It was on the Outlook Irrigation District, twenty miles northeast of Toppenish. The asking price was $24,000, with 20 percent down, owner financing.

From the first minute I saw the place, I knew the rundown little farm was exactly what we were looking for, and, more importantly, it was in a price range we could afford. Ann left work early and came down to Outlook to examine the farm with me. She agreed completely. We signed an earnest money agreement on the spot, and the old woman who owned the place accepted our offer that same night.

Ann's parents received the news of our purchase with the same stony silence they gave the announcement of our betrothal. My banker father-in-law knew absolutely all he wanted to know about farming from reading the bankruptcies that flowed across his desk at the bank, which was the state's largest agricultural lender.

They made it clear that they viewed our decision to buy a farm as their daughter's second colossal mistake, marrying me being the first. They were not comforted by our assurances that we had no intention of becoming full-time farmers, having seen firsthand how tough it was to make a living farming. Ann and I just wanted a little place with elbow room that we could call home, a small farm productive enough to allow us to "work off the payments."

Hah! Who were we kidding?

The soils on our new farm at Outlook were a light silty loam, fine as cake flour, and rockless to a depth of about twenty feet. It was on a rolling hill bordered on the south by the Sunnyside Canal, which was the first of many big federal irrigation projects undertaken by the Federal Bureau of Reclamation after the turn of the century. The enabling legislation, giving the bureau its life, forbade any one person from receiving federal water on more than 160 acres. Consequently that policy and the extraordinary fertility of the land in the valley kept the farms relatively small, many of them ten and twenty acres. Truck garden vegetable patches and high-gross crops like asparagus, apples, peaches, pears, hops, cherries, concord and wine grapes were sandwiched in between the standard row crops of corn, wheat and hay. The valley climate and the incredible productivity of the soil offered practically limitless options. Three miles from our new farm was the nearest town and our new address, Outlook, Washington.

The town of Outlook boasted a post office and a few houses with a grade school a mile or so down the road. A fire in the 1930s had swept away Outlook's boardinghouse and several other enterprises, and the town never found the energy to rebuild.

The federally financed Sunnyside Canal project was a massive improvement over the small irrigation systems which had been started by real estate promoters. Quick to recognize the lure of the land to city dwellers, the promoters had advertised the Yakima Valley to people back East as the next Garden of Eden. "Just add water and the desert will bloom in a perfect climate that produces fifty tons of water-melon per acre, and twenty tons of apples." The promoters' questionable ethics notwithstanding, Washington's Yakima Valley turned out to be one of the few places in the West where the land had the potential of living up to the extravagant claims.

Ann's tightfisted control over our purse strings and our work-for-rent agreement with the duck club in Toppenish, enabled us to save up the small down payment we needed to buy the farm in Outlook. Now we owned seven bred heifers which we had raised and were experienced in the business of raising calves, which were readily available from the many dairy farms in the valley. Our new farm had twelve acres of open land which could be planted in row crops; there were also six acres in pasture, four acres in alfalfa, and five acres of concord grapes. The soil of the open land and pasture was as good as the soil in the vineyard. The diversity of this farm made it appealing to us, it meant we were not putting all our eggs in one basket. Buying the farm was definitely a departure; we were heading off in a brand-new direction. Even though we had learned a few facts about cattle, neither one of us had ever looked at a grapevine up close before.

Even to the eye of a novice, the Outlook farm was a total mess, a "fixer upper" in real estate parlance. The former owner, an older woman named Lepha Fields, held the contract on the balance owed on the land at 6 percent interest, so we didn't need approval from a bank. We closed the deal in thirty days, and as long as we made the payments, it was ours.

After the Second World War Lepha Fields had moved to Outlook, with her husband Harold, from the mountains of Idaho. Her doctor recommended that she move to a lower elevation as the treatment for her serious heart murmur. The new climate and lifestyle of that small farm in the Yakima Valley invigorated Lepha, but at the same time, Harold went into a long decline. He was well past fifty when they bought the little ranch, and during his last years he had been so weak with heart troubles he hadn't been able to help at all.

The tiny widow struggled to take care of the farm after the death of her husband. By pure grit, Lepha had hung on. Barely five feet tall, the little old lady worked from sunup to sundown, every day except the Sabbath. Even though her place was shabby and disorderly, she somehow got the crops in. Old-fashioned in every way, Lepha recycled and saved religiously. The house, yard and small garage were filled to overflowing with jars of every description, box after rotten cardboard box of them.

Moving into the Outlook farm proved to be double duty, because we hauled one load of Lepha's refuse to the dump for every trip of our own stuff we hauled in. Just two-and-one-half years before, we had moved into the honeymoon swamp at Three Bridges with barely two pickup loads of possessions. Now, including all the farm stuff, it took about a dozen pickup loads to move.

The cabin at the duck club was a palace compared to the house we bought. Our new house was a rotting little one-story shack which had been built in three separate additions, totaling only 850 square feet. The core of the house was about seventy-five years old and built without a foundation. The root cellar under the house was well named, as the sucker roots from the neighboring black locust trees reached white and blind from the dirt-walled dugout looking for nourishment. The plumbing drain system in the house was patched with rags and flattened tin cans that were baling-wired to the spider-infested floor joists. The damp dirt cellar walls had the look of mildewed chocolate, the horizontal layers of the volcanic silts evidence of their deposit on the bottom of the prehistoric lake that so long ago covered the Yakima Valley.

Lepha's little farm had been broken out of sagebrush in 1910, decades before the house well had been drilled. The livestock watered out of a small year-round drainage ditch on the east edge of the place. Water for the house came from irrigation water stored in an old cistern underneath the front yard. The cistern was a jug-shaped affair reported to be twenty-five feet deep and about twelve feet across at the bottom, narrowing to a four-foot-wide neck at the top. The cistern had been hand dug in the hard-layered dirt and its insides covered with a thin coating of plastered cement for waterproofing. Irrigation water was run into the cistern through a homemade filter — a 16-foot cedar board flume packed with sand. Water then was pumped out of storage by hand as needed. The cistern had been large enough that, with judicious use, it would hold enough water for house use to last from October — when the irrigation water was shut off in the fall — until early March, when the canals filled again for the rest of the season.

The old cistern was in use as a septic tank when we moved in. It was covered with an old cast-iron wheel from a dump rake, rotting boards, and leaves littered from the nearby trees. I shuddered with fear the first time I investigated just how hazardous the unguarded cistern mouth was for the unwary trespasser.

Ann's boss at the bank, who noticed our industry and Ann's persistent drive to pay back all funds borrowed ahead of schedule, approved a farm-operating loan to us for $2,500. The money was allocated to buy a twenty-year-old, fifty-horse Oliver Super 55 gas tractor for $1,200. The rest of the loan would be spent on used hay machinery and cultivating equipment for the vineyard, along with a few more calves to stock our small ranch. Our plan was to take the money needed to operate our new farm right out of our "off-farm" paychecks and pay our farm bills as we went.

Even after our move across the valley to Outlook, I continued to work as a farmhand back in Toppenish. But finally, Swede and I had a blowup one hot morning while I was behind Swede's barn digging postholes and setting railroad ties in them. The project I was working on would substantially increase the size of Swede's corral facilities. Cattle prices were up, and Swede, who the year before had been named the Yakima County Cattleman, had a reputation for being hard on hired men. On the blistering morning of our first and only argument, Swede's temper flared; he thought I wasn't setting ties fast enough and I thought I was. At the end of our quarrel I quit. I admired Swede; I'd learned a lot from him and outlasted any previous hired man. This last day I'd learned enough.

The next day I got a job driving tractor for a farmer closer to home. Dwayne Van Patter was young, good looking and a relentless worker. He was farming over a thousand, leased, irrigated acres of sugar beets, wheat, cannery peas and silage corn on the Sunnyside, Outlook and Roza irrigation projects. He kept eight hired men running tractors twelve hours a day, six days a week. He told me to report at six o'clock the next morning to drive a 120-horse International pulling a roller harrow. My job was to pack the earth behind two tractors that were plowing in adjacent fields. Going back and forth between the two fields every hour, I had to keep up with both plows. Quickly packing the light soil behind the plows was vital to conserve the precious moisture for seed germination.

I told Dwayne when he hired me that I had a doctor's appointment scheduled in Yakima on my second day of work. When I got back to the field after that appointment my tractor was sitting just where I had left it four hours earlier. No one had filled in for me while I was away, and now the two plow tractors were acres and acres ahead. At seven o'clock p.m. the other tractors shut down, leaving me running alone at my chore. At ten-thirty p.m. I decided to call it a day and went home to dinner, still a few hours short of catching up to both plows. When I reported to work the next morning at six o'clock, Dwayne fired me on the spot for not staying up as late as necessary to finish the fields.

Two days after Dwayne canned me, I got another job at a feedlot on the sandy high banks of the Yakima River about five miles from our new home. Mark Arstein, the operating partner in the feeding operation, Ruehl and Arstein, assured me that I would learn every job on the place, starting at the feedmill which made the daily grain ration for six thousand head of cattle and fifteen hundred lambs.

The lamb and sheep ration was mostly ground hay with a little barley added. A touch of fat and molasses were mixed in to hold down the dust, as sheep are prone to coughing if their feed is too dry. My job was to load the mix into a feeder truck from the mill and haul it straight to the feed bunks. For the cattle, I steamrolled corn, wheat, and dry peas, and added ground hay, supplemental minerals and molasses making "cow granola." The cattle feed was hauled by the dump truck load two miles out to the cow lot, where it was mixed with corn silage. The feedlot crew worked nine hours a day, five days a week, and a half-day on Saturday, leaving me time to labor at our small farm mornings, nights, and weekends. Ann and I were jealous of every hour after dark we had free to patch up our wreck of a house.

The first job we tackled on our rat-shack was to tear out the rotting living room floor, excavate a crawl space, and wheelbarrow ten yards of dirt out the front door. The house was without a foundation; the old floor joists had just been laid right on the ground with no support stones of any kind. Due to the dry climate, the Douglas fir lumber had lasted for more than seventy years until rot overcame it. Actually, the eight layers of aging linoleum which lay on top of the crumbling floorboards were all that kept us from punching our feet right through to the ground. The roof leaked, the plumbing was shot, and the whole house was infected with dry rot and bugs, but it was ours, all ours!

At my request, Jim Ballard, the county extension agent, came out to our place and showed us how to prune our new vineyard and get the weeds under control. The neighbors were more than helpful with their suggestions on how to get the rest of our place back in shape. The ten-acre field just east of the house had gone to weeds the last year Lepha farmed. It stood chest deep in Russian thistle, the classic tumbleweed. The large, round Russian thistles are covered with small hooked thorns by the thousands, and have tough stems that make disking or plowing practically impossible. Burning is the only way to get rid of them. The tumbleweeds are held to the ground by a taproot that rots so the winds of spring can launch new generations as their parents roll across the countryside. The only way to get a good burn on the field, we were advised, was to windrow the nasty weeds into piles before they were torched.

Johnny Johnson, the elderly bachelor who lived on the farm neighboring us on the west, loaned me an iron-wheeled dump rake his dad had bought in the twenties. The dump rake tongue had been modified so the contraption could be towed by the tractor instead of horses. The trip lever also had been extended, so it could be released from the tractor seat. The rake was in workable shape, though it was more than fifty years old. It was just what the doctor ordered for my tumbleweed situation. The thistles, when stacked chest high, burned as if they had been soaked in gasoline, the fire occasionally launching sparks thirty feet in the air, blazing furiously like shooting stars.

My little Oliver 55 tractor was too small for plowing the steep tumbleweed field, so I hired a neighbor to plow under the remains of Lepha's last crop. I followed behind the plow to work the ground down with my little tractor pulling my homemade harrow. The harrow was in three four-foot sections, which I had scrounged out of a neighbor's junk pile. I wired them back together and then attached them to a black locust boom I'd cut from our side yard. It took four trips over the field with this cobbled-together harrow to work the field to a seed bed so I could plant my first crop of corn.

The soil in the field, when finished, had to be level and tightly packed so the irrigation rills would run their tiny ribbon of water down the field without breaking over into the next row and leaving dry strips. With no culti-packer or big tractor, my method was to go over the field several times, each pass at a different angle, basically packing the dirt with my tractor wheels and dragging it smooth with the harrow. The neighbors suggested that silage corn would give my ungerminated weeds seeds a better run for their money than a less-vigorous crop.

Earl McDaniels, the neighbor who farmed a small piece next to us, said he would loan me his corn planter when he finished with it around the fifth of May.

It took Ann and me all winter to prune the 2,500 vines in our five-acre vineyard. For mental recreation I started working on a novel as I pruned, the great American farming novel, to communicate to the masses what I'd been learning. Though the vineyard looked like a disheveled mess, the vines were in vigorous condition. After pruning, the canes were wrapped around and securely tied to the trellis wire. The trellis supported the vines under the weight of a crop and held the fruit up out of the way of the tires of the culti-vating tractor navigating the narrow eight-foot rows. In the early-morning light of spring, the seemingly dead grape wood of the vineyard suddenly turned purple and fuzzy as the buds broke on May third. All winter the vines had seemed brittle and lifeless, but the fast-growing shoots soon turned the whole vineyard green with young leaves, unfolding like butterfly wings as the grape shoots telescoped out.

When our first-calf heifers calved, we bought an extra calf to graft on each one. The heifers were all dairy cross stock who were producing plenty of milk for their own calves and had enough left over for another calf. Grafting a calf is easier said than done. The trick is to get a cow to accept a strange calf as her own, which, at a minimum, means letting the calf nurse at will. With her keen sense of smell, a cow can pick her own calf from a herd of thousands. Since she is genetically programmed to allow only her own calf to suck, all other calves are rejected with a kick or a head butt should they venture too close to the groceries. We tried one grafting remedy rumored to work: dousing the calves with strong cologne, hoping to confuse the cow's sense of smell. Not one out of the seven heifers was fooled.

Baby calves need to eat at least three times a day. Ann helped with their feedings before and after work and, home from work for lunch, I handled the noon feeding alone. I had built a stanchion nailed onto our cattle-feeding manger, which enabled us to lock the cows' heads when they ate their hay. All the calves, natural born and graftees alike, were kept separate from the cows, except at feeding time. Once I caught the cows Ann brought the calves in to suckle, making sure that the cows got the same calves every day. The head catch restraining the cows only partially defeated their udder defense system; not much kept them from kicking the stuffing out of anything that got close.

Just Born

The last of our seven cows to calve was a thousand-pound, black Holstein-Hereford-cross heifer. The first time I trapped her in the stanchion, she almost went nuts and came close to tearing my homemade head catch loose. Her bovine eyes bugged out as she stared back in horror as I coaxed a graftee up to her left flank. Her own calf was busily sucking on her right side, tail a-wagging. Just as I got a teat to the mouth of the graftee, the cow nailed it with a lightning-fast hoof to the head. I whacked the cow on the back of the offending leg with a "learning stick," and so the battle went, the poor recruit getting the worst of it.

Earl, the neighbor who loaned us the corn planter, had stopped by to say hi about this time. He was on his way to change a set of irrigation water in a field next to mine. Most of the farms on our irrigation project were all watered the old-fashioned way, by gravity-flow rill irrigation. Few farmers had switched over to sprinklers due to the cost of the pipe and pumping. Earl hung easily on our corral fence watching my struggling calf-grafting operation. Our cows had calved in March and April and, by varying degrees, were accepting the graftees. The cows had discovered that if I was anywhere close with my learning stick, they had better behave, or suffer swift retribution. The calves also had quickly gotten the message that they were safe as long as I was standing behind their cow. Despite my weeks of vigilance, not one of the first-calf heifers had totally given up kicking the graftees matched to them. Some, even after a month with the learning stick, stubbornly resisted. Out of the herd, only our old milk cow had readily accepted her graftees: three extra calves, one for each faucet. It was a question of who would wear down first, the first-calf heifers or me, as we battled morning, noon and night to get the calves fed.

Earl draped himself over the splintering wood of our rough-cut fir board fence and spread his broad forearms out along the top corral board. He rested his chin in a nest made with his hands.

"Having fun?" he asked.

"You bet," I replied sarcastically, as I wiped the sweat off my forehead with the torn sleeve of my workshirt, "But I'll tell you, she's not," pointing to the black baldy heifer with my learning stick.

"I knew an old guy who yoked the calf he was grafting together with the natural-born one and put them on the old cow that way," Earl said with a sly grin.

"What the heck do you mean, 'yoked them together'?" I asked.

"You can make two collars out of anything — old harness leather or even a rolled-up piece of burlap sack. The collars shouldn't be tight enough to choke the calves but tight enough so they don't slip over their heads either. Then take some baling wire or a short piece of chain and connect them about four or five inches apart. Bingo, you've got instant Siamese calves," Earl said with a laugh.

"You're not serious. How do the calves get around?" I asked incredulously.

"Well, I guess they are pretty confused at first. But in a day or two they get used to it. You know, like kids in the sack race at a church picnic. Pretty soon they can run yoked together like a bat out of hell. The cow gets so dang confused and frustrated seeing the calves yoked together, wanting to let her calf suck, but trying to keep the other one away, that she'll just worry herself down into a frazzle. After the first day, almost without fail, she'll just give up and let both of them suck. If she's a real knothead it may take two days. You just put them in a pen by themselves and let the three of them work it out," Earl suggested.

"Have you ever collared calves together yourself?" I asked.

"Nope, but we had an old Dutchman for a neighbor when I was a kid, and he did it all the time. Gosh, it was a heck of a sight seeing two calves cabled together running full speed out in the pasture."

I was getting busier and farther behind as spring marched toward summer. Any plan that might cut down my workload got a careful hearing. As it was, feeding the calves shot my whole lunch hour and ate up precious time morning and night. I was ready to try anything, no matter how crazy it sounded. A week later, I had seven pairs of Siamese calves and hung up the learning stick for good. I liked Earl's solutions.

With a few more visits from the county extension agent and the continued willing assistance and advice from our neighbors, Ann and I got through our first season of farming in pretty good shape. Earl helped me find a home for the silage corn that I planted on the tumbleweed patch. Our five-acre alfalfa field raised over thirty-five tons of hay in three cuttings to give us more than enough winter feed for our growing herd of hayburners. I had grub-hoed my guts out, and the grapes looked a lot less weedy than when I had taken them over; but they still looked trashy when compared to Johnny Johnson's grapes next door. The neighbors had warned me that if the grapes were too weedy at harvest time, it could be difficult to find pickers willing to harvest them.

The concords had set a good crop and survived my bumbling farming techniques well enough to cause the trellis to sag under their ripening weight. Long, graceful canes cascaded from the vines held up by the wires five feet off the ground. The canes sported hand-sized leaves, curling tendrils, and grape bunches slowly turning purple. The air in the grape rows was heavy with the foxy perfume that made my head light with anticipation. I picked a sample of fruit to take down to the lab at the Seneca Foods processing plant, where we had contracted our crop. Lepha had a contract with them; and when we bought the grape acreage, Seneca continued the contract with us. The agreement required that the grapes have a minimum soluble sugar level of sixteen brix (which is 16 percent sugars by weight). For each half-a-brix higher, the price per pound went up until it hit the quality ceiling at twenty-two brix. The pricing schedule made grapes which tested twenty-two brix worth about 25 percent more money per ton than they were worth at sixteen brix.

We had also inherited an obsolete picking system from Lepha. Her final year of farming was the last in which Seneca would accept grapes in the old forty-pound, wooden lug boxes. Now, the food processor insisted on receiving grapes in bulk tankers from the machine-pick operators, or in four-by-four-foot shallow bins from hand pickers that could be moved with a forklift. Machine picking was out, as far as our vineyard was concerned. Our vines were too crooked and our trellis too weak to take the punishment a machine picker dished out. My plan, since we had no access to a forklift, was to use the picking boxes that had come with the vineyard. We would then swamp them out of the grape rows on Lepha's old two-wheeled trailer, and then dump them one by one into shallow bins. Our bins would have to be filled in place and empties stacked on top until the desired configuration for hauling was achieved.

Next door Johnny Johnson was still picking the old way — into wooden boxes. He could deliver them that way because the contract he held was with National Grape Co-op, owner of Welch Foods. The grape growers owned the company lock, stock and barrel; and, as a consequence, Welch was sensitive to the needs of the smaller farmers, allowing them to still pick into wooden boxes.

The Mexican family, the Flores, who had picked Lepha's grapes the year before, showed up a week or two before harvest. She said they had enough cousins and assorted relatives to pick our grape crop in about a week. The Outlook district was one of the earliest harvest areas, so there was generally little problem getting a grape harvest crew. The migrants were done thinning the sugar beets, and picking apples were still a few weeks away. Just as Lepha had predicted, the whole Flores family showed up to pick. Every member of the large family, from the two-year-olds to the great aunt, came out to the vineyard for an inspection tour. The pay I offered was a piece rate of fifty cents a box, up five cents from the year before. The Flores family went back to their cars and discussed my proposal while I sweated out the prospect of having to get another crew together. Five minutes later they came back, grabbed the picking pans and harnesses, and we were under way harvesting our first grape crop.

I enjoyed watching Ann, who had taken her two-week vacation from the bank to be at home for the harvest, drive the tractor and trailer while I walked behind her, laying out empty boxes under the vines.

The grape picking went on without a hitch, and soon we had assembled our first straddle truckload of bins, full and dripping with pungent juice. An intoxicating aroma hung in the air around the load of grape-laden bins. The air was fanned by the wings of the hundreds of yellowjackets that came to drink the purple nectar oozing from cracked grape berries. As Ann and I watched our first grape crop head down the road to the processor, I felt a sense of loss, like saying goodbye to children that had matured and were now leaving home. The race to the grape-harvest finish began eight months earlier with pruning the vines, had now come full cycle, leaving them looking tattered and spent and in need of new trimming, almost in the same condition as I had found them when we started.

The best news of all for us in 1973 was the price of grapes, which had spiraled up to the highest point in the history of the concord market. $200 a ton was being paid cash to growers such as ourselves. This was a fourfold increase from the previous year's $55 per ton. Ann and I were in heaven! Adding our grape, hay, calf, and corn silage crops together, we had enough money to make our farm payment, pay off our equipment loan at the bank, and have money left over!

The idea that we had been able to pursue our dreams and make money to boot (all in our spare time!) seemed an auspicious sign; and when a neighbor, Johnny Johnson, announced a month later that he was going to sell his farm, we jumped at the opportunity.

Johnny's dad had carved the Johnson place out of sagebrush in 1914 and had built the two-story house in which Johnny lived. The little forty-acre ranch had provided the Johnson family with a living for more than fifty years. As a young man, Johnny had planted the first six-acre concord vineyard on a double-cordon trellis, and those vines had given him thirty-five years of excellent production. The weight slips from his most recent harvest showed that he had produced slightly more than twelve tons per acre of nineteen-brix grapes from the vineyard — a real bumper crop.

Johnny's tonnage was almost double ours. His vineyard was more than three times the age of my twelve-year-old vines, which meant they were in their peak bearing years. Immaculate care was the difference. Johnny had spent long hours making sure there were no breaks in his foliage canopy. Every vine was in the peak of health, and not even the smallest weed got a foothold. He had started a second vineyard of four acres in 1970 and trained the vines up to the trellis, ready for their first crop the following year, to be harvested by a new owner.

The balance of Johnny's forty acres was open land, all of it tillable except for about twelve acres that had been in the old soil bank and had not been farmed for years. That field needed to be leveled to be farmed successfully. However, we were assured by the Soil Conservation Service that if, after leveling, we did some subsoiling with a big ripper and laid on a healthy dose of cow manure to get the soil organisms going again, we would have a fertile field before too long at a cost of about $2,500. Due to the richness of the ancient silt loam that lay forty-five feet thick in the field, the dirt would come to life quickly with the right care.

The only problem was that buying Johnny's place was way over our heads and beyond our means. After weeks of soul searching, ambition won the battle over pride. We did about the hardest thing any self-respecting young couple can do: we asked Ann's parents for a loan to help us make the down payment. Ann's folks did not make a habit of doling out money to their kids, so we had no idea how our request would be answered. We soon learned that they were willing to help us, but before they did, they delivered stern lectures about what total idiots we were for going into farming in the first place. There was one proviso linked to their offer: they would help out with the down payment if we could find financing on the balance.

The increased workload of our new expanded farming operation required me to quit my job at the feedlot. At the peak of our first summer in Outlook I had been working 120-hour weeks. The new farm would easily eat up the fifty hours a week I was putting in at the feedlot. My mother offered to help out and loan us $5,000 for the soil conditioning job on the Johnson place and to buy a few more pieces of used equipment we needed to expand our operation. The bank, based on our past record, agreed to write us a new operating line of credit.

We were now deep into the farming business.

4

The More You
Wiggle
The Deeper You
Sink

Spring turned into summer with deceptive speed. I planted soft white wheat on most of our open land and corn on the freshly leveled field we had reconditioned. Collaring the grafted calves worked like a charm again the second year. By double-cropping our cows with graftees, we were able to raise almost twice the pounds of beef that we could have otherwise. The price for steers, after years of being in the basement, rose to more than fifty cents a pound. Higher prices, in turn, upped the demand for the baby dairy calves we were buying, and their price nearly doubled from $45 up to $80 or so. Losing a calf to pneumonia or scours was now a serious loss.

My younger brother, Kurt, who had not been doing well at community college, came out from New Jersey to live with us for a year. Both my mom and I hoped that hard manual labor on our farm might change Kurt's outlook. To make sure that with his extra help we would stay fully busy, Ann and I rented another five acres of grapes. They were owned by a neighbor lady who, due to poor health, just couldn't farm them anymore. Her vineyard was in even sadder shape than ours had been when we took it over from Lepha. But we were optimistic.

With our sharecropping arrangement on the five acres, we were farming a total of twenty-one acres of concord vines with the potential to raise 200 tons of grapes per crop year. The way I figured it, if the grape prices held one more season, we would make a killing. Ann, of course, tried to damper my enthusiasm with far more conservative projections. She hoped we would make enough to pay for all the things we bought to farm our extended acreage: a second tractor, sprayer, flatbed truck, baler, mowing machine, and hay elevator.

Like many a farmer, I wish I could have seen what was in store for our grape harvest.

My used equipment was continually falling apart, which necessitated buying a welder and a line of shop tools to patch things back together again. With Kurt's help, we started to make progress on building a new corral to replace the hodgepodge of rotten flume lumber and baling-wired livestock pens that were Lepha's legacy. Our new corral was to be built with railroad ties and rough-cut two-by-eights. I dreamed of the day when I could put a cow in a pen and know that when I returned to the corral in the morning, I'd still find her locked up.

We were lucky to avoid the effects of a big spring windstorm. Central Washington windstorms can be fierce. In fact, they're so fierce that spring winds have blown moving, loaded trains off their tracks! Gusts have launched buildings like box kites. In our valley duststorms were not uncommon due to the cake-flour texture of the silt loam soils. In early April we experienced a two-day blow that peaked at seventy miles per hour and wrenched several mobile homes off their pads near Toppenish. The wind came when farm crops were vulnerable. Nearly all the fields in the Lower Valley which were to be planted to row crops that year had seed already in the ground. Wheat, peas, and sugar beets hadn't yet produced much, if any, ground cover. The howling winds dropped visibility to zero as countless tons of soil and young seedlings blew away.

The fine dirt poured through the cracks in the walls, until our house was choked with dust. So much dust settled on the living room rug that walking across the room left footprints in a sea of soil. This was a homemaker's worst nightmare; the grit got into everything. When the duststorm finally let up, the road at the mouth of our driveway was filled with two feet of sand. Roads all over the district were blocked by drifts, some as high as six feet. Other than the colossal housecleaning disaster, our farm escaped damage. Some of our neighbors weren't so lucky, and had their spring crops sucked right out of the ground or their equipment drifted over with the fine powder.

Though we avoided serious damage from the spring windstorm, we weren't so lucky with the freeze that descended on us on the morning of May 14, dropping the temperature below twenty-four degrees for several hours. As the sun rose, the entire Yakima Valley was covered with a haze of smoke from the tens of thousands of oil and propane heaters that had been warming the county's 70,000 acres of fruit trees all night long. Approximately a million gallons of fuel were burned to save the fruit crop that night. Most of the heaters were lit from eleven o'clock on.

The next step was to assess the disaster to our crops. It didn't take long to discover that our vines, which had new shoots about eight inches long, were wilted. In the hazy morning light, the shoots looked as bedraggled as if someone had run a blowtorch down the grape rows. The grapes at our place and those that Johnny had nurtured looked almost destroyed. Worse were the new shoots in the rental vineyard, which was forty feet lower in elevation. There, the young grape leaves hung like stir-fried lettuce from chopsticks. In a single stroke, our hopes for an entire year were wiped out. The grapes, our biggest cash crop, were gone!

The following night, the mercury again dipped down to twenty-four degrees. Again the valley floor glittered with sputtering flames and smoke to hold back the cold. Nearly every orchard heater that could be found in the valley was lit in an attempt to save the crop. Like me, most of the valley's grape growers had been caught off guard. Just one or two vineyards out of 15,000 acres in production had frost-control equipment. The danger of frost damage normally was so slim by the time grapes budded out that virtually no grape farmer invested the money for prevention. But this year, the gambler's odds had paid off in the other direction; the grape growers had rolled snake eyes.

A week after the frost, when the coffee-shop moaning had subsided somewhat, it became obvious that not all vineyards had been hit equally hard. I put a micro-nutrient fertilizer spray on the vines where the damaged grape leaves showed signs that they were struggling to revive. Down on the rental vineyard, however, the loss was almost total; there were no signs of life anywhere.

Because a grape bud contains three growth chambers — the primary bud, the secondary bud, and the tertiary bud — there is often a chance for survival after frost damage. The secondary buds activate when the primary bud, with its fruiting and leaf structures, is destroyed by frost, wind, or bud worms. However, the secondary bud fruits at only 30 percent of the potential of the primary bud. The tertiary bud is activated only if the secondary bud also is destroyed, and it is a leaves-only survival cane.

The vines at our place slowly came back to life. We crossed our fingers and hoped a grape crop would set. The rented vineyard on crop shares, however, was going to be a whole lot of work for damn little crop, but we'd see it through to harvest, paycheck or no. Luckily, our February-planted winter wheat hadn't yet headed out and wasn't damaged by the late freeze; the corn, only barely up, was also unaffected.

If the grape harvest struck a mortal blow at our budget, it was a Godsend that President Richard Nixon removed the federal price controls on wheat, which for many years had been artificially set at about $1.85 a bushel. The unfettered world grain markets took off like a runaway stagecoach. To the farmer's good fortune, when the U.S. government got out of the wheat-buying business, the Russian government got into it, and made the biggest wheat purchases in our agricultural trading history. Wheat prices soared to an all-time high of $6 a bushel.

A few weeks before grain harvest, I bought a beat-up '62 Chevy two-ton flatbed truck with a hoist. Kurt and I built plywood-and-pipe grain racks for it. We decided to buy the old truck to save on our crop-hauling bills, which were beginning to be substantial. The $1,800 truck seemed like a necessary move. Our wheat was to be thrashed by a friend who owned an old, open-platform John Deere 55 combine with a twelve-foot header. He also would supply a grain-hauling truck. While he ran the combine, I would drive both trucks, leaving one in the field to be filled while the other one was on the road to the elevator. Our wheat fields looked beautiful. The grain heads were full, with plump, wheat kernels. The neighbors all agreed the crop looked like it should do better than one hundred bushels to the acre, a bumper crop of wheat.

The combine operator's grain truck was a '54 International in even worse condition than mine. The twelve miles back and forth to the elevator, were slow and touchy. I drove praying that the rolling junkpile would finish the trip without breaking down. The truck's bench seat was worn clear through to the springs. The seat's stuffing had been replaced with a nest of burlap sacks that were filthy from years of use. The door on the driver's side was always flying open whenever I hit a pothole, crossed railroad tracks, or if it darn well felt like it. The two-speed differential was practically gone, making shifting a nightmare.

On the way to the elevator the second day of wheat harvest, hauling a full load, I missed a downshift in my friend's International. No matter how much I ground around with the shifter, I couldn't find second gear. I pumped the brakes as I slowed to turn right at an intersection. Then in the middle of the turn, the driver's-side door flew open.

I pumped the brake pedal for all I was worth, because coming into the same intersection at the same time was a station wagon full of migrant workers. I finally gave up trying to grind the truck into gear and devoted my attention to avoiding a crash. We were passing close enough that I was in danger of taking out their windshield with the driver's-side door that had swung wide open. Hanging onto the steering wheel with one hand, I grabbed blindly for the open door with the other. The inside door panel was entirely missing except for the window crank. The vent window was gone also.

When my fingers finally found the door, seconds before impact with the crowded station wagon, I grabbed it by the frame and slammed it shut with all my might — on my thumb! A quarter of a mile later I brought the grain truck to a full stop. I missed the station wagon entirely, but in my blind hurry to shut the door I smashed my thumb between the door frame and the jamb.

My thumbnail pounded like a jackhammer. With each heartbeat, a blast of pain shook my central nervous system. Holy smokes, it hurt! I sat there immobilized a few minutes, as the tidal wave of pain crested. My thumbnail was still intact, though there was a deep crease where it had met the door frame. The ragged flesh around it was protected by the thumbnail, which had taken most of the abuse. There was some bleeding from under the nail, but there was not much I needed to bandage. My thumb hurt a hell of a lot more than it looked like it should. After a few more minutes, the searing pain settled down to a loud pulsing reminder to never, ever do that again.

I put the old truck in gear and drove onto the elevator. I was reasonably sure that the thumb wasn't broken, but it hurt enough to wonder why not! The rest of the day I drove holding the wheel, thumbs up, trying to refrain from touching anything with my throbbing digit. During two more truckloads to the elevator later that afternoon I managed to only bump the aching thumb once or twice.

By evening the thumb was beating like a war drum. I took a few aspirin when I came in at the end of the day, but to no effect. Lying on the floor with my arm up in the air didn't help either. By eleven o'clock p.m., the throbbing pain from my thumb was so intense I finally called the emergency room at the hospital for advice. The doctor on call explained that the pressure from the blood trapped under the nail was causing most of the pain. He said that if I didn't want to come in to have the procedure done in the hospital, I could try a home remedy. The remedy involved heating a paper clip on the kitchen stove, hot enough to melt a hole through the damaged nail. The hole would release the trapped blood to relieve the pressure and cut the pain dramatically. The doctor said that the blood would absorb the heat from the paper clip as it went through the nail, so if I was careful and didn't push the searing metal rod down into the meat, there was little chance of hurting myself with the procedure. I was desperate! I was willing to try just about anything.

Ann, sympathetic and helpful, found a paper clip and turned our electric stove on high. On the first stab, the paper clip just sputtered unsuccessfully as it melted a small divot in the thumbnail. I put the paper clip back on the burner for another go, as my thumb pounded with increased pain. A second, third and fourth try still did not achieve a blood-relieving meltdown. The extra pressure on my thumb for each unsuccessful attempt practically had me in a frenzy. I gave up and headed in to the hospital.

The emergency room doctor took a hospital-issue paper clip and heated it over a Bunsen burner. The clip was glowing red hot in a matter of seconds. With a puff of smoke, the glowing paper clip went through my nail like a hot knife through butter. About two tablespoons of blood erupted from the small crater in the thumbnail, and my pain subsided immediately. Our electric stove at home hadn't heated the paper clip hot enough to do the job, and it hadn't occurred to me to go out to the shop for the torch.

Two days later we finished grain harvest. Our wheat crop came in at ninety-seven bushels per acre with a cash price of nearly $6 per bushel, almost triple the price of two years before. We could make good money growing wheat at those prices!

If the price of wheat was the highest in peacetime history, tit was a different story for the frost-damaged concord grapes. The market price was shaping up to be a lot less than the record price of $200 per ton that processors paid the year before. Three of the valley's processors announced their offers in August, ranging from $120 to $140 per ton.

The processor we were contracted with, Seneca Foods, held out. This made us nervous; we didn't know what to think. Seneca still hadn't announced the price they were paying for grapes on September 10, ten days after harvest began. We started picking the grapes on Johnny's place first, because they were contracted with Welch. The grape prices only marginally affected the price Welch paid since it was a co-op that operated on the grower's capital. Welch paid for the crop in a complicated formula that tied the price to how well Welch performed as a business and spread the money out over almost ten years. Though their payment program would leave us cash short, I was happy we had Welch to deliver to. I was not about to harvest and deliver the portion of my crop to Seneca until they announced their price.

The frost reduced the grape crop much less than feared on both our place and Johnny's. I didn't look forward to picking the rental grapes, however, which were carrying only about one-third of a normal crop grown from the secondary buds. We planned to skip our Seneca grapes and move to these poor grapes next if Seneca still hadn't announced their price when we finished harvest at Johnny's. We stood to lose part of our harvest crew when we moved to the rented grapes because the fruit was so sparse that it would be tough, if not impossible making good money picking them.

The day before we finished the grapes at Johnny's, Seneca announced to the newspapers that they were going to pay only $60 per ton! My heart sank, and Ann and I were furious. The announcement threw the valley's grape industry into a tizzy. The Seneca growers had every right to feel bushwhacked, since many of them had delivered their crop before the price announcement. The growers expected Seneca's offer to be similar to the $120 to $140 a ton the other processors were paying. The published Seneca price was half what everyone else was paying! The other processors saw Seneca's price as a declaration of war.

Seneca offered to release from their delivery contracts all the growers who did not like their price. The company had planted 1500 acres of concord grapes seventy miles east of the valley on the bluffs above the Snake River in partnership with the Spiegel catalog family from Chicago and Pete Tagaras, one of Washington State's biggest farmers. Their vineyard was just coming into bearing, and it seemed obvious that Seneca wanted to get rid of the pain-in-the-but little five- and ten-acre growers, like myself, who started them in the grape business in the first place. Despite Seneca's treachery, we had two things to be thankful for: one, Welch offered to take all the grapes from growers like us who had split contracts. Second (though it may sound like sour grapes), we didn't pay taxes in the port district that provided those SOBs from New York a home for their processing plant.

At the price Seneca was offering, we wouldn't come close to covering our total expenses. The costs just to pick our grape crop, were nearly $35 a ton, plus a few dollars more to haul them to the juice plant. Even though we'd have to wait a long time for the money, the Welch contract was a lifesaver to our small enterprise.

Now, our finances were stretched to the limit. The $30,000 of income we budgeted to come from our grape crop was first cut severely by frost, then put out of reach by the Welch deferred payment schedule. If you'd been a customer of Welch's for years or were near retirement, the Welch payment schedule was perfect. But for overextended, cash-poor farmers, like ourselves, it was the pits. All of our other crops — wheat, hay, corn silage, and cattle — had done reasonably well that year, with very good prices. But the farm budget Ann and I submitted to the bank at the beginning of the year didn't resemble reality. The lack of grape cash plus the strain of the second land mortgage and the payments on the expanded fleet of junk equipment became a heavy weight dangling over our heads.

After Thanksgiving, my brother went back East, to our mutual relief. The year had been good for both of us, and now it was good that it was over. The farm workload had slacked off with all the year's crops coming in and, alone again, Ann and I started to prepare for the coming year.

During the following winter Ann and I had thousands of vines to prune. She was still working full time at the bank, so I had her help only on the weekends. The hundreds of hours spent pruning in the vineyards gave me time to contemplate not only my novel, but what we had gotten ourselves into in our headlong rush to become full-time farmers. We had moved out to the country to escape the ratrace of the city and taken up farming as a way to have employment near our home in the country. Now, I realized, we were on a treadmill moving at a pace those city rats would never believe. The demands of the six-crop rotation and livestock operation kept me working seven days a week year round without letup. I could never really go home from work because it was always looming as close as my boots at the back door. The crop diversity possible in the valley gave a true workaholic everything he could ever dream of. The thing that was really frightening to me was that I was starting to like it.

I found that I thrived on the constant pressure of having to weave two dozen different tasks into each day's work. I didn't mind spending ten to twelve hours a day on the tractor cultivating corn or cutting hay in addition to the chores with the livestock and irrigation. Keeping the irrigation water moving and getting every inch of my fields wet with gravity-powered water was an art that I took seriously. The amount of water that we received was just barely enough to get around the whole farm once a week, which, in hot weather, was not fast enough.

The first year of being totally self-employed and farming full time was the first time in my life that I had ever been fully challenged. Ann was double-timing it also. I could not have given one more ounce of effort, or worked any harder if I had a gun to my head. It was exhausting, but the feeling of accomplishment fed my stamina to accomplish even more. In December, Ann and I took our first full weekend away from the Outlook farm since we'd bought it two seasons before. It was like a strange awakening to go to Seattle and see people who drifted through life working only forty hours a week. After two days in the city, we were both dying to get back to the farm.

Not long after we returned, I received a lesson in carelessness that I would long remember because it could have ended much differently than it did.

It was Sunday on a February morning that began like any other: damp, grey and overcast — a perfect day for burning. The continuing chore of cleaning up the accumulated trash from Lepha's tenure on our place, even after dozens of loads to the dump, was, after almost three years, still a work in progress. On this Sunday, I gathered a big pile of wet, rotten lumber and assorted debris and then made a fateful decision I would regret every minute for the next weeks. The barrel with diesel in it was in the back of the pickup down at the bottom of the hill, but the gas tank was only thirty yards away. I chose the gas.

My plan was to drench the burnpile with gas and then start it going from afar by throwing in a lighted ball of newspaper. As I bent over to light that newspaper, I failed to notice that a very slight breeze had just come up from the direction of the burnpile ten feet away. I took off my gloves and got a book of matches from my shirt pocket. I struck the match, and KAWOOF!! The fireball from a gasoline vapor explosion engulfed me. I hit the ground immediately, rolling away from the flaming trashpile, trying to put out my burning coveralls. My head had been mostly protected by a heavy leather cap, but my hair sticking out around the edges of the hat was also aflame. When I came to a stop against a tree five yards away, I was singed but no longer on fire.

I quickly unzipped my smoldering coveralls and, while struggling to take them off, I realized my fingers were shrieking with pain. Looking down, I saw that the skin on the backs of my hands was peeling off in sheets. I ran to the house for help, bursting through the living room door like an emissary from hell. My hair was wild with burnt frizz, my face was beet red, and my eyebrows were completely gone. I was hunching forward cradling my ruined hands, roaring with pain, when, in total shock, Ann looked up from her vacuuming.

Panic quickly gave way as Ann assessed my injuries. My hands were my only body parts that were seriously burned. They were bad, very bad. Ann peeled off my charred coveralls with as much care as possible. I became nauseous and lightheaded with the tidal wave of pain that followed and slumped into a kitchen chair. Ann filled a stainless-steel bowl with ice and water for my hands, then called the hospital emergency room to tell them we were coming.

During the ride into town, the stay in our quiet little country hospital, and then the trip to the burn center at Harborview Hospital in Seattle, I spent the time running and rerunning in my head the stupid mistake I had made of using gas to start that fire. The five minutes I had saved because the gas tank was closer than the diesel barrel was spent ten thousandfold later in agony enhanced with the realization that I could be disfigured and disabled for the rest of my life. And there was no way to redo my idiotic decision.

Back at the ranch Ann had chores to do, cattle to feed, grapes to prune, on top of caring for me in the hospital and her full-time job at the bank. Only two weeks before my accident she discovered that she was pregnant with our long-awaited first child, and now the full weight of our communal responsibilities rested solely on her shoulders.

Eight weeks after being burned, the tender new skin on the backs of my hands and fingers finally stopped cracking and bleeding. Except for a few small spots of third degree, the burns had all been less destructive, with the promise of full motion, full recovery, and little scarring. For a long, long time I'd have to wear gloves when I worked to protect the new skin which would tear easily, but I was lucky. I came through this brush with hell without any permanent damage.

Thinking about my punctured thumb and now my burns, I realized why farming is one of America's most dangerous occupations. What with tractors to roll over on you, livestock to trample you, hay balers, combines and corn choppers to tear your limbs off, it was a lucky farmer who survived a year without an accident. I concluded that, of all the hazards, the farmer himself was the most dangerous.

For a number of reasons, Ann and I became persuaded that a partnership with a farming couple we knew would be a good idea and would give me some free time to work on my book. After all, four people would be more productive than two, we decided. As a first step, the partnership decided to hold onto the grapes Ann and I rented the year before in hopes the sad crop would be followed by a bin buster. Sherman Schaffer, a neighbor to the east of us, stopped by one Sunday afternoon and offered to sell us his fifty-two acres that lay immediately adjacent to our farm. He wanted only $6,000 down and the rest on a personal contract. Schaffer's doctor had advised him to cut back his farming operation or suffer the consequences. The reason he wanted so little down payment was that he had already sold another big piece of property and wished to avoid paying any more taxes that year than necessary. He was offering us the property with a down payment as low as the cash rent we would have paid had we been leasing the land instead of buying it. We jumped at the deal.

The four of us decided to buy the land as a partnership. Ann and I lifted the down payment out of our already approved operating line at the bank. Operating our farm the year before had cost $56,000, and we figured that by tight budgeting we could sneak by the whole season using the $6,000 until the crops came in and I confessed to the bank what we'd done.

We traded the old Johnny popper in on a new $6,500 fifty-horse Oliver 550 with a loader to load our grape bins onto our flatbed truck for the trip to the processor. The 550 was the same tractor as the twenty-year-old Oliver Super 55 with only a few exterior sheet metal changes. All the implements we owned that fit the old tractor would fit on our new one as well.

Our farming partnership proved to be unworkable. By the end of August it was obvious, if we were to remain friends, we couldn't be in business together. All four of us decided that after the grapes were picked, the partnership would end. I couldn't wait! My idea of decreasing my own work through the benefits of the four-power partnership had proved to be a joke. In just eight months my work on our sixty-seven acres had been doubled to include all the work on the combined 120 acres.

The whole crop year, while our partnership fell apart, Ann grew larger and larger carrying our firstborn child. She was officially due the end of September, but she determinedly hung on until we got through grape harvest the first week of October. Without regard for her advanced state of pregnancy, she drove tractor in the vineyards and the flatbed truck delivering grapes to the processor throughout the harvest. Ann's mother Betty finally couldn't stand the wait for her long-overdue first grandchild and came over from Seattle to wait in person for the baby to be born. The day she arrived, Betty rode along with Ann on the last trip of the harvest to Welch's delivering our grapes.

To say that Ann's mother was concerned about her daughter working so physically hard would have been an understatement. She was convinced her grandchild was in jeopardy bouncing down the road in our rickety flatbed truck. Ann's belly was so large it nearly got in the way of her turning the oversized, non-powered steering wheel. Despite my mother-in-law's anxiety, they arrived at the

Welch plant without incident. Betty got out of the truck first and paced the blacktop, waiting for Ann to struggle out of the truck cab and undo the cables holding down the loaded bins moving with the ponderous slowness of full-term pregnancy.

Betty flagged down a forklift operator and told him, just as Ann shifted her watermelon stomach out the driver's-side door, that her daughter was three weeks overdue and could have the baby right there in the yard if they didn't snap to and get our truck unloaded. Betty's instructions to the plant crew were delivered with such authority that they immediately took over the task with the cables and bin irons and had the truck unloaded in record time.

The morning after the last load of grapes were delivered, Ann's waters broke, and twelve hours later we were the proud parents of a beautiful seven-pound, seven-ounce baby son, Blake.

Grape harvest 1975 was over.

With our ill-fated partnership ended, I dropped the lease on the sharecropped grapes. It was a burden I didn't need, and on top of that it wasn't making us any money. The winter job of pruning 10,000 vines ourselves was obviously more than I could do alone, now that Ann's time was taken up with more important duties. Ann and I agreed we'd hire some help, so one late January day when the two Hernandez brothers stopped by the farm asking for work, they were hired on the spot.

I had met the brothers five months earlier when they had pulled their mufflerless Chevy off the road at our vineyard during grape harvest looking for work. My policy was that if field hands stopped and asked for work during harvest, and I had any picking pans that weren't being used, they were hired, no questions asked. I wasn't an immigration agent or a border guard, I was a farmer with a job that needed doing. And they needed work. We put our heads together and solved both our problems. Almost all of the people who applied to pick grapes at our farm were Mexican. I didn't ask the few whites who applied for jobs if they were citizens, nor did I ask the Mexicans.

The Hernandez brothers had worked our entire twenty-one-day harvest season making $60 to $80 for a six-hour day working their butts off picking grapes. They each could pick about twice as many grapes as I could in the same amount of time. I assumed they were fresh from Mexico because they didn't speak a word of English.

"Put more grapes in the bin" was the only Spanish I knew. The Hernandez brothers stayed with me through the three-week grape harvest, and by the end we each learned some of the other's language. The Hernandez boys were so honest, happy-go-lucky, and hard-working that I couldn't help but like them. When we finished our grapes I found them a job picking apples at the neighbors.

The brothers finished pruning our grapes in February, but in March, Easter weekend, they stopped by again. This time they were the three Hernandez brothers. I was glad to see them again and to meet their younger brother. They were all fresh from their native village in Sonora, where they had lived like kings for a few weeks of midwinter vacation. They had built their ailing mother a new house with the money they saved from their work foray into the States. I felt badly; I had no work that I could offer them at the moment. I knew that the job prospects were slim that time of year for field workers. All the farmers had completed pruning, and asparagus had not yet come on. Other than tractor-driving jobs, work in the valley was as scarce as hens' teeth.

I sensed their dejection when I said, "No work." But being the day before Easter I couldn't just send them away empty handed. My own people, just a few generations before, like the Hernandez brothers, had been immigrants struggling to survive in a new land. My conscience searched for a solution.

Our farm was in an out-of-the-way place, just the perfect kind of area for people to dump off their unwanted cats and dogs they couldn't bring themselves to deal with. Homeless pets, in a seemingly unending procession, wandered up our driveway looking for a new home. One day some weeks before, there had been a new twist to that old story. A peahen had walked up the driveway and found our half-dozen chickens scratching in the yard and immediately installed herself as boss chicken. No neighbor had claimed the big, obnoxiously loud bird. The peahen had been in residence for about a month and had become a real nuisance. She loved the cat food and shat daily on the front porch, making it a minefield we had to negotiate to keep from tracking peahen puckey into the house. Her favorite roost was sitting on our chimney warming her tailfeathers over the updraft from our woodstove. The mortar holding the chimney bricks together was old and rotten, and just that morning the peahen had kicked a brick down the chimney, which blew wood ashes and soot all over the living room. The peahen flew up to our shaky chimney as I told the Hernandez brothers to wait while I got something in the house. The youngest brother almost jumped out of his skin when I returned to the front yard with a shotgun.

"No, no, no," I said to calm him, and pointed at the peahen. "Your Easter dinner!"

With so much of our income coming from the deferred Welch payments, we relied on the other crops to carry us and our obligations. Wheat prices were good, though not as high as the year before, but cattle fell by twenty cents a pound, our silage corn crop yielded over thirty tons per acre at the same price as the year before, and the hay crop was excellent, with prices at about $65 per ton. Ann and I were fully on the credit treadmill now. Even with her paycheck from the bank, where she returned six weeks after Blake was born, and with me running full speed on the farm, we were barely making ends meet.

In 1976 we farmed alone. With the exception of hiring help for the little plowing we needed, as well as buying labor for some of the grape pruning, Ann and I did everything else ourselves. We had been surviving on Ann's take-home wages, which we knew were not going to last forever, now that our family was started. I was working sixteen hours a day and not yet taking any wages out of the farm we were building. If we could hang tough and keep building, our operation soon would be big enough that Ann could come home for good to full-time motherhood.

The more I reflected on our daily dilemma of paying the bills, the more disgusted I got. Here I was, doing 95 percent of the work on three farms which a generation earlier had each been self-supporting units, providing for three different families. Now I was farming them all, and I had to send my wife out to work in town to make ends meet. I suppose my attitude was responsible for our gamble and plunge into triticale.

As diverse a place as the valley was, new crop alternatives were being tried every year as farmers continually searched for ways to control their destiny. Most new crop trials involved only a few acres. But normal caution was gone with the wind when a company from Amarillo, Texas, sold a reputable grain and feed dealer in Prosser on the vast, untapped future of triticale.

Triticale was a cross between wheat and rye, "the grain of the future," its proponents said. Triticale was high in protein and lysine, an essential amino acid in short supply in other grains. Its flavor when mixed with wheat flour in baked goods was fantastic. The outfit from Texas was offering lucrative contracts for triticale production in the Northwest. The contracts were competitive with what a farmer could make growing wheat. In February I decided to plant forty acres of triticale, and so did enough of our neighbors that in a few weeks there were 4,000 acres of triticale in the valley under irrigation.

The grain grew lush and thick like wheat, but the forage was much denser. It was a beautiful crop. When the triticale was ripe it stood a full six feet tall, with grain heads like giant golden bananas. Too bad the grain heads were half empty.

The promoters from Texas went broke before the Washington crop of triticale was ripe enough to harvest. The 150 farmers who had grown it under contract were left holding the bag — a specialty crop without a market. To sell our crop of triticale for feed grain, which was the only commercial market, was going to be a disaster. On top of that, since triticale seed from Texas was not adapted to the Northwest growing conditions, it didn't yield worth a damn. Most growers harvested about 50 percent of the grain tonnage that wheat would have produced on the same ground.

The irony was that triticale flour was great stuff. Mixed one-third to two-thirds with regular wheat flour, it made breads, pie crusts and baked goods of all descriptions that were simply delicious and wholesome as well. The main problem with triticale was that nobody had ever tried it before, and with a name like that, who could blame them? Ann and I bought a stone-buhr electric home flour mill to experiment with the new grain and were soon selling ten- and twenty-pound sacks of the freshly ground triticale flour right out our kitchen door.

The *Yakima Herald* heard about us and did a full page story on triticale baked goods on the front page of their Sunday foods section. Half the page was a color photo of Ann, standing next to a wooden table I'd made, overflowing with triticale baked goods fresh from Ann's oven. Our phone rang off the hook with orders for nearly a week. We eventually sold a few thousand pounds of flour, a couple pounds at a time, before we gave in like most of the rest of the snookered farmers and sold the balance of our triticale crop for cattle feed.

Our fourth season farming in Outlook, we raised 172,000 pounds of grapes, 140,000 pounds of sweet corn for Del Monte, 240,000 pounds of hay, 120,000 pounds of triticale, 120,000 pounds of dry grain corn, sixteen feeder steers and a dozen butcher hogs, and still I had to send my wife to work in town to make ends meet.

Always alert for additional ways to squeeze money out of our operation, we rented ten acres of our farm to a mint grower for a share of the mint oil crop. The Yakima Valley is the nation's primary source of natural mint oils for gum, toothpaste and candy. Mint is swathed like hay, then green chopped into a special wagon to be towed to the mint still. Most farmers who grew mint had their own stills or shared one with a neighbor. The aroma around a mint cooker, and for a mile or so downwind, was pungent. In the pre-herbicide days, growers used wing-clipped geese tightly fenced on small pieces of a field to keep the mint weed free.

The first year we lived at Three Bridges, the mint oil business in the valley was devastated with prices as low as $3 per pound, far below production costs. The price crash had placed many big growers into bankruptcy proceedings in 1971. The first farm auction I ever attended with my Toppenish neighbor, Glen, was held to pick over the bones of a busted mint grower. Five years later, mint oil had soared in price. In 1976 short supplies had driven the price up to over $20 per pound! The few mint farmers left were clearing unheard-of profits of $1,000 per acre growing mint oil! As a comparison, good irrigated wheat grossed only $500 per acre and netted perhaps only $150 per acre after expenses.

Generally, land values had been creeping upward along with the rising inflation of the '70s. Lower valley land prices were soon charging upward, fueled by the demand created by mint growers with fresh, hot money in their jeans looking for good farm ground to buy. Several of my older neighbors saw the opportunity, sold out, and retired. The farm sale prices were astonishing compared to prices only two years previous. Land values had been driven up 300 percent over what we had paid for the same kind of property four years earlier. The idea of selling our farm was tempting. The more I thought about it, the more appealing the idea became. I discovered I had an aptitude for farming, but the high-speed, squirrel-cage pace of the Yakima Valley was not what I was looking for.

When I figured the paper profits of selling our Outlook farms at the booming values and compared them with the figure I came up with to farm an equal amount of money out of the soil, I kept coming up with the same answer. The little voice in the back of my head kept saying, "Take the money and run!"

Weighing heavily in favor of selling was the fact that
Blake, our firstborn, was taking all of Ann's spare time. She
could no longer drive truck and prune grapes with me.
When she went back to work at the bank just weeks after
Blake was born, she felt guilty every morning when she
dropped him off at a babysitter on the way to work. Ann had
quit her demanding job as production manager at the Union
Gap branch of the bank and transferred to the branch in
Sunnyside only six miles away from our home. The change
was for a job with fewer demands so she could concentrate
more on motherhood. Her work at the bank was supposed to
be temporary, or so we thought five years earlier when we
lived on the reservation. Ann had not taken a teller's job in
the first place with any idea of making a career in banking
like her father. Starting a family was the thing Ann had
chosen as her highest priority, and she was quite willing to
derail her banking career to pursue it.

5

The Breaks Ranch

. . . .

Heaving like a winded elephant, the take-up chains, gears and bearings on the ancient combine header were straining to tear the twenty acres of corn ears from their stalks. A yellow river of grain poured into the combine hopper as the tough little machine shuddered and popped as it shelled the heavy crop of corn.

Even though I was driving as slowly as the combine allowed, and slipping the clutch, things started breaking. First it was little parts, like chains and belts, then a strawwalker plugged, tore loose and battered the insides of the combine. Next, the feeder chains on the header started flying apart. The dense foliage of the bumper crop of corn was simply too much for them. On average, fighting the constant breakdowns, I spent at least one hour repairing for every hour running. I grew to hate that damned old combine with a passion. This harvest that should have taken a few days dragged into four weeks of frustrating aggravation.

Finally, with only four acres of the cornfield left to go, a bearing froze and a shaft heated, crystallized, and broke, tearing up practically everything in the vicinity. The two-row header was now a one-row header, and no replacement parts were available. I was down to harvesting one cornrow at a time. The November winds blew dry corn leaves in my face as I sat clattering and huffing down the last row of stalks. Freezing my buns off on the open platform of the combine, I swore a solemn oath that I was never going to use this stinking machine again. The choking cornstalk dust had made long hours on the combine respiratory agony, and the constant repair work, with the parts flying off every few hours, made running the machine a curse that forced sizzling epithets and black profanity from me. I was going to trade the miserable combine off with my very next machinery purchase, or get a stick of dynamite and blow it to hell. Or, better still, sell the whole farm, kit and caboodle, and buy a cattle ranch up in the hills without a cornstalk in sight.

In mid-December we went on a Sunday drive south over Satus Pass to the Goldendale Valley, about 1,400 feet in elevation above the Columbia River. The average rainfall in Goldendale was about fifteen inches per year, double the precipitation in the Yakima Valley. The Goldendale Valley was composed of open farmlands surrounded with timber stretching to the north and west to the glacier-covered flanks of Mount Adams. To the east and south were the dry grass-covered, windswept Columbia Hills, concealing the glorious view of the east end of the Columbia River Gorge just a few miles beyond.

As we drove into town, we were taken by Goldendale. In 1976, it was a neat, little town with two grocery stores, two tractor dealerships, and all the storefronts on Main

Street filled. The air was crisper and cleaner-smelling than the more heavily populated Yakima Valley we'd left fifty miles behind. The log trucks parked in town were evidence of a much different environment than the sagebrush desert of Yakima only a few miles away on the other side of the mountains.

The ranch we were going to see, led by a talkative real estate salesman, was a thousand acres. It had farmable ground of about 600 acres which constituted a peninsula surrounded on three sides with deep canyons, the Breaks. The Klickitat River was to the west, the Little Klickitat River to the north, and Swale Creek to the south. The ranch-house and barns sat in the middle of the property in a small private canyon three miles from the nearest neighbor. The soil maps in the real estate listing packet showed several hay and grain fields that were all each well over a hundred acres each in size. The ranch's non-farmable acres were timber, scab rock, and steep canyon-side hills.

The Breaks Ranch felt wild, as free and majestic as the red-tailed hawk that sailed above us in the winter sky. A line of a dozen deer disappeared into the oak thicket below us. This ranch was so different from our busy little farm in Outlook. I loved it! Ann and I looked at each other; I knew from the expression on her face that she was crazy about the place too.

During the drive back to Outlook over Satus Pass, through cow country where we had helped Swede and Glen, and past the wildlife refuge where we had slapped mosquitoes while we lived at Three Bridges, Ann I hashed over our options. The Breaks Ranch was where we wanted to be in ten years; it was where we wanted to raise our children.

In the Lower Yakima Valley, cash-flush mint farmers were fueling a red-hot real estate market for good farm ground. Buyer demand was so intense, I was positive we could have our farm sold at a huge profit in less than a month. Our fields in Outlook were all Class I land, suitable for any crop imaginable. We also had senior water rights from one of the oldest irrigation districts in the Yakima system. Several of our older neighbors had sold their farms that fall, and from them we got a close estimate of what our farm would bring on the booming real estate market.

The real estate salesman in Goldendale had come right out and told us that the owners of the Breaks Ranch were desperate and would take far less than they were asking. Farmers Home Administration, the holders of the mortgage, was breathing down their neck. The ranch had been on the market for two years without a serious offer, and with the depressed cattle market, there were damn few people even out looking for a farming operation of its type.

"Go ahead and make him an offer, any offer. The owner is finished, damn near busted. He has had it! Make him an offer," the salesman urged like a broken record during the ranch tour.

The Breaks Ranch looked like heaven to me. In my mind's eye, I could see the winter wind creaking through the giant pines, swirling down into the rushing Klickitat River Canyon. My imagination soared. Every waking hour for the next few days, all I could think of were different scenarios for unloading our frantic Yakima Valley farm for the wheat and cattle ranch up in God's own hills.

Over the next few days, Ann and I schemed at the possibilities of selling out. We could instantly turn the real estate price inflation in the valley into equity, simply by trading farms. The irrigated land in the Yakima Valley was going for all-time-high prices; the cattle ranch in Goldendale, on the other hand, was a bargain-basement deal

Breaks Ranch and Mt. Adams

because the cattle business was in the tank. Operating money, however, would be needed to buy 100 head of range cows to stock the place and a different line of farm equipment for the vastly larger fields. The picture became clearer and clearer in my mind that this was our golden opportunity, our big chance to sell high and buy low. It was our admission to the Capitalist Hall of Fame.

Dryland farming is considerably more laid back than irrigated farming. There were windows of slow time in the winter that last for months in ranch country. The pace of ranch life would be the pace of the seasons, very different from the three-ring circus of diversified farming we were running in the valley. I looked forward to running range cattle, spending hours on horseback, and to hell with the miniature tractors and pruning the grapes. The timbered canyons and wide-open mountain scenery of Goldendale was where we wanted to be. And best yet, by just closing the deal we could trade our rathole of a home in Outlook for a substantial four-bedroom, two-story ranchhouse with its own private canyon.

This dream, of course, was contingent on whether we made an offer that the owners of the Breaks Ranch would take. There were still many questions about the ranch our novice real estate salesman was falling all over himself to find answers for. He was doing his very best to grease the wheels to get the deal up to the cash register. Every time he called with more information, he stressed again that the sellers would be willing to take far less than the asking price.

One week after we'd first seen the Breaks Ranch, we were back in Goldendale with our offer. That was the moment when the broker took over. His name was Joe, a huge man with a fifty-plus-inch waistline and a loud, booming voice to match. He reeked of cheap cigars and the lunch special served that day at the local cafe. Joe assured us that he would personally go out to the ranch that evening and explain our offer to the sellers. But he said he was doubtful they would accept our offer, being so far below their asking price.

"If that isn't enough money," I said, as Ann and I were walking out the door, "you'd better find another buyer." I put as much finality into my voice as I could muster.

Driving out of town, Ann said to me, "If they don't take the offer, the heck with it! As a farm, it is not worth one penny more. In fact, as beautiful as that ranch is, I'll be relieved if they turn us down."

At nine o'clock that evening, Joe called. "You bought it," he growled over the phone line.

"They signed, as is? With no changes?" I asked.

"Yep, they went for the deal just the way you wrote it up. I've only been back to the office five minutes; the ink on their signatures is not even dry yet. The sellers would like to close the deal in thirty days, but with FHA involved you never know. It could be months, but FHA wants this farm sold badly, so they shouldn't be too much trouble. You just bought yourselves a ranch," he barked back through the phone.

I gulped hard as I hung up. "Hot damn!" I muttered as I propped myself against the refrigerator. We really had bought it.

"Oh, Honey!" Ann said, beaming, as she put her arms around my neck with a devilish grin spreading wide across her face. "We've really gone and done it now!"

We both broke into a fit of uncontrollable laughter. It was too good to be true. What we'd just done was too scary to be true. I found a bottle in the back room and broke out the fancy wine glasses we'd gotten as wedding gifts but had scarcely had an occasion to use. We toasted ourselves and our new adventure and raised our glasses to other poor suckers who would soon (we hoped) be living in our rattrap Outlook farmhouse.

A day later, Joe Rogers called again.

"Are you sitting down?" he asked.

The beautiful four-bedroom house on the ranch we'd bought had just burned to the ground! The night after the sellers signed our earnest money offer, the beautiful old Victorian house had gone up in smoke! Totalled! Gone! Completely destroyed! While the family had been watching TV that night, the TV's power had gone out. Checking the fusebox, they had found the wall was on fire. Their kids had been in their pajamas, ready for bed. In a few minutes of freakish confusion, after a call to the volunteer fire department twelve miles away, everyone bundled up and ran out to the family car to wait as their beloved home spewed a flume of sparks into the winter night sky. Moments after they had gone outside, fire broke through the dry cedar shake roof. The guys from the volunteer fire department arrived in time to see the roof cave in. The fifty-year-old wooden house was a bonfire that burned with the heat of an inferno and, doing so, consumed everything the family had accumulated in fifteen years of married life. The firemen saw to it that the fire didn't spread to anything else, but that was all they could do. The house was gone before they arrived. Joe Rogers, the broker, wanted to get together with us as soon as possible to discuss our options.

Ann and I were stunned. Our two-day mental joyride had come crashing down.

Several days after we recovered from the initial shock from the torching of our future home, Ann and I decided to bow our necks and go ahead with the purchase anyway, regardless of the obstacles. Charge ahead, house or no house. We agreed that the house had not been the reason for buying the ranch in the first place. It had been just a fringe benefit, the icing on the cake. We were buying the ranch for its wild, rugged beauty, its timber, and the crop potential of its 600 tillable acres, all of which were untouched by the fire. What came next, the renegotiation with the tragedy-struck sellers for a new purchase price for the Breaks Ranch, minus ranchhouse, was the hardest business dealing of our lifetime.

The ranch family had gone through several bad years in a row as their farm failed. It added insult to injury to have their house burn up with everything they owned, just as they were on the edge of selling and getting out of their untenable position. Even though they were in one hell of a tight bargaining position, Ann and I found we didn't have much heart to use our advantage. We negotiated a value for the vanished house at near the insurance coverage, deducted it from the agreed-on purchase price, and got ready to close the deal.

Our own Outlook farms, right on schedule, sold at very satisfactory prices to mint growers attracted by the irrigation rights that went with the purchase.

It was spooky to go out to the Breaks Ranch with the house gone. The chimney was all that was left standing. The half-basement was a mass of twisted pipes, charred appliances, and ashes; it gaped like the wound of a freshly extracted tooth. The only human artifact to survive the fire intact was an old Indian stone grinding bowl sitting on the hearth. It had been found in one of the fields the first year the last unlucky owners had been on the place.

The small private canyon, in which the homestead was set, felt infinitely more wild and far less hospitable than it had seemed with the ranchhouse in place. A bitter winter wind blew across the site as Ann and I looked down at the ashes of the death of one dream and the birthplace of another.

The winter of 1977 finished with the lowest snowpack on record. Drought was the subject of every coffee shop conversation, with predictions that it might be the worst one on record. In early February, there was a dry corn snow falling when we arrived in Goldendale to sign the closing papers. When Ann and I walked into broker Joe's back office in the old hotel, the pungent fumes from three over-flowing ashtrays and the smell of stale beer from the containers strewn around the room were strong — remnants of a poker game the night before. We got down to business immediately and soon signed the final papers.

As anticipated, we felt the strong chill of disapproval from Ann's parents when we announced to the family our change of farms. They were happy that we had made a "killing" in real estate, but they thought buying a cattle ranch with the profits was as wrongheaded as buying a farm in the first place. Ann's mother scheduled an inspection tour for early March. I tried in vain to put the visit off, having her wait until we started the new house. Both Ann and I felt the sight of the charred house ruins on a narrow gravel road fifteen miles out of a small town was not going to be a big hit. Betty insisted on coming anyway, determined to see where we were planning to take her one and only grand-child.

Betty, though a banker's wife, was not stuffy nor formal in the least. She was raised in Texas and Oklahoma. Her father had invested in a large ranch in New Mexico, where she had bagged a mountain lion at the tender age of twelve. Her formal education in the East at Foxcroft and Vassar had not dulled her love of the wilderness. After World War Two, she met and fell in love with a dashing young naval officer, freshly decorated with the Navy Cross, earned on the beaches of Normandy. He brought her to Seattle. Ann's future father, Bill, shared Betty's appreciation for the untamed world and encouraged her trips, which included helicopter skiing, trekking the world's backcountry, and scuba diving in the Galapagos Islands.

When Betty arrived in Outlook for the drive to the Breaks Ranch, Ann and I informed her that she had another grandchild on the way. Betty, always a gracious guest, skipped the chance to tell us what poor timing we had.

The early-spring drive over Satus Pass to Goldendale was icy and treacherous. At Goldendale we were met with a blustery west wind and snow showers on the wet pavement. About halfway out to the ranch from town, I glanced down at my gas gauge. It was riding on empty. Quick mental calculations showed that there was no way we could drive the remaining seven miles out to the Breaks Ranch and the fifteen miles back to town on the meager amount of fuel the needle was showing.

I announced to my passengers that we would have to make a U-turn and find some gas. I knew from our roadmap that Centerville was closer to where we were than Goldendale. Centerville was the mailing address of the Breaks Ranch and the site of the grade school our children would attend. Ann and I had never seen Centerville, so as a face-saving measure I suggested rather than to go back to Goldendale, we'd take a sightseeing detour into Centerville for gas and find a treat for our cranky one-and-a-half-year-old Blake, who was squirming in his carseat.

There was no gas to be bought that day in Centerville. A tiny old gas station stood empty and boarded up on the main intersection of town. Judging by the faded paint, the station had been closed at least a generation. The town was comprised of a dozen or so scattered houses, a combination post office/grocery, a grange hall, a volunteer fire station, and the school. In the parking lot of the aging two-story, brick schoolhouse we turned around to go back the way we had come. We had no choice but to go back to Goldendale for gas. As we drove back down Centerville's Main Street, coming towards us, propelled by the strong spring winds, was a ten-foot-long piece of old rusted sheet metal roofing. It came ka-flop, ka-flop, ka-flop right down the center of Main Street, headed east. I waited as the roofing passed us, trying to come up with some funny comment but couldn't think of one. My mother-in-law, Betty, was silent for the rest of the drive back to Goldendale and out to the Breaks. She stared icily out the window. I knew what she was thinking, and it wasn't complimentary.

Like any young couple, Ann and I wanted a much bigger house than we could afford. We settled on a plan to build a large shell, finishing it, room by room, over the next ten years. Ann and I soon found out why most couples who build a house together end up divorced.

The dry winter of 1977 turned into the Drought of 1977. The rainfall was only one-eighth of normal, by far the driest year on record. Our first year's crops on the Breaks Ranch were a disaster! The 200 acres of dryland hay didn't even get tall enough to clip! Our wheat crop came out at a poor eighteen bushels per acre; and if the drought wasn't bad enough, the price of wheat fell from a high of $6 per bushel a few years before, to a measly $2.85. At the same time the costs of production had soared.

We bought fifty head of mother cows to run on our range, such as it was. The herd was one-half the number of cows I had been led to believe the ranch would support, but with the dry weather the grass was so short that there was barely enough feed. The drought gave me few farming chores; so looking at the bright side, it was a great year to build a house. By August, we and our small crew of friends and family had the house closed in and a roof on. We had moved out of the borrowed sixteen-foot camp trailer that had been our home for five months and moved into the basement of the "Monster" with the sawdust drifting down through the cracks in the floor from the construction going on upstairs. A single cold-water tap was jerryrigged from the remains of the former house's water system. We had extension cords for power. Life in the construction zone with our curious toddler, Blake, was not exactly according to Dr. Spock, but we were living through it. All the while, as our construction project stumbled forward, Ann got increasingly larger, due to deliver our second child in early October.

Soon after we bought the Breaks Ranch we met our closest neighbors, Earl and Helen McClintock. They lived only three miles away and were in their fifties and childless. Earl McClintock was as different from Earl McDaniels, our old neighbor in Outlook, as night was from day. Earl from down in the valley was big and robust, always with a smile on his lips and a kind word for everybody in the world. Also, he was sober as a judge. None of those terms applied to our new neighbor Earl. Both Earl and Helen were small and wiry, neither one any bigger around than a fencepost. They owned the 2,500 acres immediately east of the Breaks Ranch and Earl and his wife worked fourteen hours a day, seven days a week, raising cattle, hay and wheat.

With our house burned, the wiring normally supplying electricity to the pump in our spring house didn't exist. So for the first two months of work on the Monster, by their invitation, we hauled all our drinking water from the McClintocks'. During this time, Earl and Helen's approximately two hundred head of Hereford cattle were in the midst of spring calving in the forty acres surrounding their house. During calving, Earl and Helen lived with their cattle twenty-four hours a day. Every other evening, when I'd arrive to haul another barrel of water, regardless of what work was at hand (short of delivering a calf), Earl and Helen dropped whatever they were doing and put on the coffee pot for a visit. The longer the better. Earl had a brilliant mind, was well read, and had intellectual interests far beyond farming. He had come to Klickitat County in the fifties to work on the construction of the John Day Dam across the Columbia River. Helen was his second wife, and together they had built quite a ranch. Their life was their work, and their work was their life. My regular visits were only a brief respite from their constant labors.

Both Earl and Helen were scrupulously honest and had no time for anyone who was otherwise. Through scrimping and saving and working 365 days a year, they had amassed a sizable operation which included three other large parcels besides the one next to us. By working almost nonstop, they were able to run their ranches with only one hired man, a quiet old gent, who was even older than they were.

With no children and no family in the vicinity, their cattle were the focus of life. As a former anthropology student, I had read incredulously how the Indians of the Great Plains who kept herds of hundreds of horses had known each and every horse by sight. Not only did Helen and Earl know all their cattle by sight, they knew who was who's daughter and granddaughter, even though there were no ear tags to identify them.

The McClintocks always moved their cattle on foot, never with horses and dogs as I'd been accustomed to over on the reservation. In fact, they didn't even have a horse on the place. Moving their cows down the road to their Centerville farm, seven miles away, Earl led the cows with a few bales of hay in the back of their beat-up pickup, and tiny little Helen walked behind the entire herd of cattle, alone, armed with only a switch to keep them all moving. Somehow, beyond my comprehension, she always got the cows, calves and bulls to their destination and never lost one. Their kindness and gentle behavior around their herd was a marked contrast to the cattle prod and hard leather approach I had learned at Three Bridges.

The first time I helped Earl and Helen in their corral, I yelled at an uncooperative cow and smacked it with a stick. Helen was mad at me for a week, probably madder than if I had whacked Earl instead. The McClintocks were as hard as nails in many other ways, but where their cows were concerned they were total softies. They never even butchered one of their own animals to eat, preferring to buy their meat in town.

Earl's thriftiness was once a cause for words between us. He showed his Scottish heritage in anything he did concerning money and was famous locally for his shrewd and frugal business head. When it came to spending money on himself or Helen, he placed the word "tight" into another dimension. He ruled household spending and everything else with an iron hand, and when he was in his cups, he was a tyrant. He and Helen rarely left their place, except for dire necessity, to go into town. I had never heard of them going farther from the ranch than The Dalles, and there only once

Helen Moving Cows

or twice a year. I doubted if Helen had ever been to a shopping mall in all her life. She bought her shoes at the grocery store and wore the same tattered winter coat all the years we knew her.

One day driving down the road as we were passing by, Earl flagged me down to ask, "Say, you wouldn't happen to have one of those small syringes?"

"What do you mean, those little two-and-a-half-cc syringes for treating pink eye?" I asked.

"Yeah, I need one for Helen," he said. "She needs a shot of penicillin," he continued, fingering a large vial of the cattle drug laying beside him on the pickup seat. The sheepish look on his face told me that even though it was midmorning, he'd been drinking.

"What the heck is wrong with her?" I asked.

"She's got a bad tooth. It's infected and all swollen up," Earl said, cupping his hand to his jaw to illustrate the location and size of Helen's abscess.

I was stunned. He was dead serious about giving Helen the shot. I suppose I should have given Earl some brownie points for not having already used the standard livestock fifty-cc syringe with fourteen-gauge needle on Helen, but the more I thought about it, the angrier I got.

"No, I don't have any of the little needles," I blistered back at Earl, "and I wouldn't give you one if I did have, you cheap bastard." I paused. "For Christ's sake, take Helen to the dentist! If you don't, I will."

Earl took my harangue calmly, and then said with a shrug, "Yeah, maybe I should." He started his truck up and started slowly off for home.

As tight as he was, he was always ready to help, like the time the following winter he loaned us his calf puller. It was the last day in February, a Sunday, and it was raining as usual. When I went down to the barn, I found a young cow lying down in the midst of calving, and even from a distance I could tell things weren't going right. I discovered small hooves upside down protruding from the cow's hind end, meaning the calf was coming backwards. I ran up the hill to the house to tell Ann.

We were in great danger of losing the calf if we didn't act immediately. A backward delivery took more than obstetrical chains and two strong backs. This called for a handwinch calf puller, a device that resembled a sturdy, steel pushbroom, with a piece of six-foot-long steel pipe for a handle. The broom part was inserted up against the cow's rear, and bolted to the end of the handle was a small come-along with five feet of steel cable to hook to the chains on the calf's legs. We didn't have a calf puller, but Earl and Helen did. As I roared up the hill in my pickup the three miles toward their place, Ann called ahead to tell them I was coming.

When I got to McClintock's Corner, the mouth of Earl's mile-long driveway, he met me coming from the house. He had the puller in the back of his pickup. I quickly turned around, and he followed me down the hill to my barnyard, with me driving as fast as I could go down the narrow rocky road.

Ann was waiting for us at the barn. We went to work immediately. After ratcheting in the cable inch by inch and using the long pole end of the calf puller as a lever, five minutes of the utmost exertion produced half a calf. I had no doubt that the calf was dead by this time, and we had to complete the job quickly or we'd lose the cow as well. After a few more minutes' effort, the calf's shoulders and head cleared the pelvis, and the calf plopped out, limp and slimy with mucus from the birth. He lay still and motionless on the muddy ground.

Ann and I sat on the tailgate of our truck completely exhausted, covered from head to toe with blood and amniotic fluid. The cow was struggling to get to her feet, her hindquarters partially paralyzed. She finally regained her feet, a very good sign, after such a delivery. Earl, all this time, had been leaning easily up against the side of his pickup, watching us work, smoking cigarette after cigarette with his work-gnarled fingers. As I loaded the puller back into his truck, he said, his words slurring slightly as he spoke, "Sorry I wasn't much help," he began, "but you know, Sunday's my drinking day...."

He gave me a perfectly sweet smile, got back in his truck, and slowly headed for home.

Our first crop year on the Breaks Ranch was a total disaster. The farm books showed we lost nearly $30,000, a substantial share of the profit we'd made selling the farm in Outlook. Many a sleepless night, as I lay next to Ann, who I was sure was working too hard for a woman so close to childbearing, I was haunted by the crushing fear that we had stepped off the deep end in our move to the Breaks Ranch. The prefab part of our house had gone up quickly, but it was a long way from being truly habitable. The hard frosts in early October made life in the basement of our drafty, unheated, construction zone more and more unbearable.

Davey's birth was as difficult as Blake's had been easy. After a week of false starts, our second son was finally born. After the hospital delivery, Ann spent one night back home in the unfinished Monster, and then left to go to Seattle to stay with her mother for a few weeks, leaving me to install the plumbing and woodstove with no family distractions.

Instead of the normal sixteen inches of rain, the drought of 1977 dropped a mere two-and-one-half inches on our ranch for the whole crop year, September to September. Perfect weather for construction work, but for ranching it was just plain lousy. Our new cattle had a tough year on tight feed. They were also on a strange pasture, half of which ran straight up and down, and with all the stock ponds dry our cows had a steep two-mile hike down into a canyon to a spring for the only drink of water on the leased summer range of 2,000 acres. All things considered, though, the cows brought in a decent calf crop, with steers weaning at an average of 520 pounds.

Just as I was starting to wonder if it would ever rain again, it started sprinkling Thanksgiving week.

We were expecting a houseful of company for the holiday. The Monster was still under full construction. Davey, our number two son, was a month old. Ann and the boys were back from Seattle now that I had installed a woodstove and hooked up the plumbing.

The woodstove was the first of three I had planned for the house. The chimney to service the other two stoves wasn't built yet, so we would have to get through the winter with just one. I had cut four cords of wood, a two-year supply, for the rattrap down in the mild Yakima Valley, but winter out on the Breaks was going to be a different matter. Our new house was five times larger and not fully insulated or even completely closed in yet. To keep our new baby warm I began burning wood like it was going out of style. I figured we would use up the last of our whole supply just keeping the Thanksgiving guests warm. But I planned to get out in the woods as soon as our company left for eight or nine more pickup loads of fuel, what we'd need to carry us through the winter.

6

You Can't Eat the Scenery

• • • • • • • • • • • • • • • • • • •

Along with building our house, I had been working off the farm weekends at a construction job for some extra income and, consequently, I was behind on all my chores. Thanksgiving morning it snowed twenty inches, and then it changed to rain. It rained in torrents the next three days, and as the snow melted, the ponds and long-silent creeks on our ranch sprang to life. For the first time since Ann and I bought the Breaks Ranch, the sound of water gurgling over rocks filled the air. One hundred yards from our house a seasonal creek rushed down the canyon. Around a small waterfall up the creek, moss and lichen sprang to life with the winter moisture. The sound of rushing water was everywhere, just as weeks before, the deathrattle sound of the wind rustling the brittle drought-damaged vegetation had been all-pervasive.

Like champagne, bubbly flowed everywhere across our fields and woodlands. The Thanksgiving deluge rendered my two-wheel-drive pickup helpless. I got stuck twenty feet off the road during my first wood-gathering trip after the rain stopped. Since it turned our clay soils to jelly, there would be no more driving in the woods until a freeze. Without being able to drive into the forest to make firewood, I soon used up every dead tree standing anywhere near the road. The next major snowstorm came a week later, and winter closed in for good.

From September all through that winter, I worked every weekend down in the Yakima Valley. A friend of mine was building a house in Toppenish and hired me to pound nails for him.

Joe Bailey was a master carpenter and a workaholic who, besides his full-time job as head carpenter for a local construction company, had a twenty-acre concord vineyard that he tended in his spare time. When his grapes were laid by in the fall, he started construction on a small spec house which he would finish working on the weekends and sell before spring. I jumped at the opportunity to take the job with Joe, because lacking carpentry skills had become a major stumbling block on my own building project. I stood to benefit from some schooling at the hands of a master.

Joe and I worked nonstop from seven-thirty a.m. till noon. He laid out the work so flawlessly that I never had time to even to go to the bathroom until lunch. Joe's credo in life was, even if you were only making $2 per hour, if you worked enough hours, you could still get ahead. He was the living proof. Joe's carpentry lessons immediately started to pay off at home. As I worked for him and learned, I cursed the mistakes I made on our house which could easily have been avoided, if I had only known what in the hell I was doing when I started.

It continued to rain and snow until New Year's Eve, when the mercury plummeted to minus ten. The subzero cold snap hung in for the first two weeks of January. I was feeding our cows at an old barn with only half enough bunk space for the animals. We owned no four-wheel-drive truck or big tractor and wagon to haul feed to the cows out in the fields. Feeding the cows required human labor to pack ninety-pound bales one at a time up the hill behind the barn to feed the livestock too low in the pecking order to secure a place at the feed manger. Day after day it was the same cows who crowded in to the stanchion, where I fed hay first. And day after day it was the same cows who waited, bawling, for me to drag their feed up the hill. While I was away on the weekends working construction, it fell to Ann to get the cows fed. She not only had to buck the bales, but at the same time she had to contend with our newborn baby and a toddler.

In February, the cold snap broke and the rain started pouring again. It rained unceasingly for days, as if to appease for the drought the year before. Our cattle suffered, as day after day of cold, pelting rain beat down on their backs. The cows started to calve in mid-February, and in our ragtag corral, not much better than the one that came with Lepha's place in Outlook, I waged the battle of calving 1978.

The incessant rain kept up until mid-March while we fought the scours and pneumonia. Losses eventually amounted to 15 percent of the calf crop. We tried everything to save them; we even resorted to housing sick calves on straw under heat lamps in our unfinished basement. In all the time we had raised dozens of calves in our little calf operation in the valley, we lost only three, but in our first calving season at the Breaks Ranch we lost four times as many. It was heartwrenching to battle for days to save a calf, then at the midnight feeding find the calf flat on its side with its eyes rolled back and the last bubbles of life captured in mucus on its grey nose. On the day we finally turned our cows out to green pasture, we had exactly fourteen bales of hay left on the whole ranch. Never in my life was I so glad to see spring come.

In the late spring we went into the cattle business big time. Ann and I bought thirty-five more cows with calves at their sides. Ann's mother, newly divorced and looking for an investment and a tax writeoff, also bought forty pair that Ann and I would run on shares for her. Our pasture was better than I could have imagined. The winter's deep snows had given the grass life that had been missing the year before. The cows and their babies were soon sleek and fat after just a few weeks of being turned out on range. The winter illnesses disappeared as they roamed the hills coated with velvet green. The canyons on all sides of the Breaks Ranch echoed with the sounds of rushing water, joined by thousands of little frogs singing their mating songs. The lichen and moss clinging to the basalt field-strewn boulders were a dozen shades of green.

In our backyard, flocks of recently returned mountain bluebirds conducted their mating rituals. The sunlight flashed off their iridescent blue feathers as they perched on top of the mossy cedar fenceposts. Pairs of bluebirds danced up and down the fence rows surrounding the barnyard as they played tag from post to post. Two bald eagles roosted in the tall pines west of the barn and picked over the remains of our very last calf to die.

Our family finances were stretched as thin as the hay carryover in our barns. As of yet, the financial outlay of building up our cattle herd and the 300 acres of new alfalfa we'd planted were consuming capital, rather than producing any. The reality that we were also starting to borrow money to live on was more than Ann could bear. She started to look for a job.

One of the unique features of Klickitat County in the 1970s was that we had a one-man, hermit FM radio station. KCIV was the only FM station in the entire Columbia River Gorge and the only radio station of any kind in our county. It broadcast from the studio transmitter high atop The Dalles Mountain on the southern border of the Goldendale Valley. The station antenna towered over the tiny studio and living quarters, which sat alone on the crest of the Columbia Hills, 3,200 feet above the river.

The radio station was owned and operated by Les Cummingham, a honey-throated baritone who lived at the transmitter site for over a decade, all alone on the top of the mountain. I listened to Les hour after hour while working on our house. His was the only FM signal we could receive at the ranch with any clarity due to the topography of the Columbia Gorge. Les fascinated me. He was the radio equivalent of a one-man band. He was on the air from nine o'clock in the morning until ten o'clock at night, six days a week, and off the air on Sundays. After a few days of listening to him, I began to realize that he did most of his commercials ad-lib. It was like a time machine; I was listening to old-time radio live from a mountaintop in the middle of nowhere.

Les played different kinds of music. In fact, any music qualified for air time on KCIV as long as there were no drums or electric guitars on the recording. He played a lot of pure junk, only barely better than Muzak; but at times he also played great stuff: classical, jazz, blues, country and folk.

Les was stricken with polio as a child, and lost the use of both his legs. He got around his small studio on the mountain in a rolling office chair. With his leg braces locked, he could make it painfully slowly, hand over hand, along the woodwork to his living quarters, an Airstream travel trailer, adjoining the studio. The trip of twenty or thirty feet from his studio to his kitchen and bedroom in the trailer required a full two or three minutes. For Les to break for lunch, he placed a full record album on the turntable, started at the first cut, then headed for the trailer. The trick was for Les to remember the last song on the record, because the thirty-foot trip back to the controls and the microphone took that long to complete.

Ann went to work for Les after his sales manager gave him brief notice that he was quitting to take another job. The disruption to Les's life represented by the loss was tremendous. Les never went off his mountain. In his handicapped condition he was dependent on others for transportation and supplies beyond the limits of the radio station compound. His specially equipped '56 Mercury was no longer in running condition, and without his sales manager as a lifeline, Les was adrift.

On a chance trip looking for cows up that lonely mountain, when I mentioned to Les that my wife was looking for work, he hired Ann on the spot, sight unseen. The following Monday she went to work for Les, training for one day with the exiting sales manager.

In her first three months, Ann tripled the radio station's meager sales revenue. Occasionally I substituted for Ann at the radio station office when she needed time for her duties as a mother. Working at the radio station was a welcome change of pace from chasing cows. I found I enjoyed selling ads and creating advertising for the station customers. Les didn't mind that we were job sharing. He was grateful he had found a dependable team who could sell, write advertising copy, and pinch hit where it was necessary.

Les's only other contact with the outside world, besides Judy, his fiancée; Ann or me, was an occasional face-to-face visit from some pilgrim who came to visit the station, or the garbled voices that came in on his CB radio, which he used to communicate with Ann. Les was far too frugal to install an expensive radio phone when he could get by with the hiss and static of his twenty-four-channel CB on the cheap. Ann soon began to hate that unreliable damn CB, frustrated with trying to weave the day's business needs in through the pop and the flutter of the static.

In the meantime, the bottom had dropped out of the hay market in the spring of 1978, with prices plummeting from $70 down to $45 per ton. With the wet winter and spring, my hay yields were great, but market prices weren't much better than the cost of our production. We planted a hundred more acres to hay on land that had been in wheat for years and years. My remaining grain fields were in summer fallow, to be planted to winter wheat come fall.

Cattle prices took a welcome jump to $1 per pound for 600-pound steers in the fall of '78, the highest price in history. When we sold our weaner calves we received almost as much for the calves in the fall as we had paid for the cow-calf pairs earlier in spring. With Ann's weekly paycheck from the radio station and the fat calf check, the domestic economy on the Breaks Ranch felt like it was starting to stabilize. The price of hay was still the pits, but with money from the calves, we were able to make some headway with our huge notes to the bank. Then winter hit.

The thermometer dropped to minus fifteen and held there for a week. The New Year came in with a snow, followed by more snow, followed by even more snow. For much of the distance, Ann's thirty-five-mile cross-country commute to work in The Dalles to sell radio time was on lonely gravel farm roads miles from any houses. Due to the heavy snows, these roads were mere tunnels of ice carved through vast fields of white. Ann had to dig her car out of a snowbank more than once while our two little boys fought in their seats. For two months the drive through the winter fog on snow-packed roads never got above freezing.

Les, snowed in up on the mountain, was getting desperate. Due to the drifts he hadn't had a supply drop in seven weeks, and he was running low on everything. He had been living on Spam and soda pop for a month, but vittles were not his first concern. He was nearly out of cigarettes! Les had gone to rationing his smokes after the fourth week of bad weather, but now he was scraping the bottom of the barrel.

The huge drifts on the steep road coming up to the station made even snowmobile travel hazardous. Ann, as sales manager, was responsible for figuring out how to get the rations to the mountaintop. Once a day, a federal worker drove a Snowcat to the FAA beacon a mile down the ridge from the station, but when asked to assist, claimed that he couldn't help unless it was a bona-fide emergency. By week seven, Les was convinced it was a real emergency: he was down to his last twenty cigarettes.

As the eighth frigid week went by and the weather still hadn't broken, the FAA man gave in, allowing Ann and our friend Carroll to ride up to the top of the mountain in the Snowcat across crusted snowdrifts that blocked the access road and made any other means of transportation out of the question. At the FAA beacon, the women shouldered backpacks full of Les's needed supplies and hiked the final mile across the snowbound ridge to the station.

Les was as happy as a kid on Christmas Day to see them. He hugged the cigarette cartons like a long-lost friend. After the supply drop, Ann and Carroll hiked down the mountain through deep snow five or six miles to the nearest neighbor, a large cattle ranch, where they'd left their car.

By spring, Ann was at the breaking point at work. Les was getting increasingly difficult with his demands and petty gripes. For her, the burden of being Les's only window on the world and the mother of two toddlers at the same time was too much. The daily commute was murder, because when the ice melted, the mud came on and miles of gravel road became soft and spongy from frost heaving. Waves of guilt crashed over her every time she dropped our two boys off at the babysitter. It knifed her to the quick that our children were being raised most of the day by a person who was not their mother, while Ann worked to keep food on our table.

As hard as we toiled, the ranch started to slip behind again on its obligations, as expenses exceeded income. We had never yet been actually late on a payment; those we couldn't make we refinanced, each loan gobbling up some more of the inflation equity that we had made from our farm down in Outlook. The Breaks Ranch simply sucked up capital like a sponge. The corrals needed replacing, the barns were rotting because they had no foundations, and the costs of establishing 600 acres of hay and grass were almost $25,000 just for the alfalfa and grass seed alone. We realized that our ranch did not have any good farmland, and that its highest productive use was to raise cows and cattle feed.

Again, there was an ulcer developing in our household, and this time it was Ann's. The pressure of our debts, and poor crops, or poor prices to pay the bills, kept us both tossing and turning at night. While I struggled to keep our livestock going, she struggled with our finances to keep our farming business alive. Together we fought with the larger and the even more gnarly problem of whether we had a realistic chance of making it on the Breaks Ranch, or if we were going to go broke just like the last owners. I think we were beginning to understand the heartbreaking economics of farming and ranching in America; it was an occupation fraught with ups and downs; it demanded too much of the will and backbone of the men and women who worked the soil, for a return that was often chancy at best.

Our faithful, long-time banker from Sunnyside was asking more pointed questions each time we went to see him. Each time those questions were getting harder to answer truthfully. We knew with a sinking feeling that it was easy to make the mistake of overstaying your welcome on a farm, and then have to watch the bankruptcy receiver end up with everything you'd worked so long and hard to put together.

The critical question neither Ann nor I wished to face was when to cut our losses and sell out while we still had something left. We knew we had become emotionally involved with our dream house, the Monster, now 35 percent finished; and the Breaks Ranch, a piece of land we had come to respect and love. We didn't want to leave, we didn't want to give up, so instead we roasted over the coals of painful choice, unable to make up our minds. I think we both were banking on a miracle, while at the same time we knew the odds were long against it.

In April it started. Ann announced she was pregnant again. We both hoped this would be the daughter we longed for. Parenthood was by far the most rewarding and enjoyable undertaking of our lives, and we were thrilled at the prospect of another child. Ann was full of anguished guilt about working while Blake and Davey were little. Her heart had repeatedly told her that her place was at home, with her babies. With a new one on the way, she was determined she wasn't going to repeat her performance with the first two children.

"After this child is born," she declared one evening, "I am not working outside anymore. If we can't make it without my paycheck on this damn farm, we'd better do something else."

"What do you mean, do something else?" I asked. "Sell the ranch and me get a job in town?"

"Whatever it takes. Get a job and we can keep part of the ranch and sell the rest of it. I don't care what we do, but all I know is that when this baby comes in November, I am not going back to work, and that is final. I am not letting anyone else raise this baby!" She gently held her belly and started to sob. "You're going to have to figure out what to do. I've given this damn stinking farm the last drop of my blood!" The pain of all the hardships of the past came pouring out of Ann in a flood of tears.

I felt guilty, frustrated and mad that we'd reached this point in our lives.

After the winter's snows melted, the howling winds of spring blew without let up. March brought no rain, and neither did April. The wind continued to blow until it dried up most of the remaining soil moisture before my hay crop even had a chance to grow. In May the weather suddenly turned very hot and then the hay struggled until it ran out of juice. On the fields with deeper soils the hay crop was fair. But most of our soil was only three or four feet deep to bedrock and there the hay crop was light and spindly.

While I wrestled with what to do about our shaky situation, I took on some custom work for Earl and Helen and sharecropped on a nearby farm which a California developer was splitting into twenty-acre parcels.

The mini-drought of '79 had brought hay prices up to $65 a ton, but for us on the Breaks Ranch, the higher price was only a tease. Our yields were so low that there was no way we were going to have any spare hay to sell. I was just hoping that we would put up enough hay for ourselves, so that we wouldn't have to buy it to feed our cows at the new higher prices.

Between our own, the sharecrop for the "mini-ranch" owners, and the custom work, I had more than 900 acres of hay to harvest. Dryland alfalfa hay is challenging to put up. The biggest problem was that the entire hay crop was ripe at the same time, making quality hay a race against the calendar, the weather, and breakdowns while I tried to get the crop up in good shape. I had traded our mower, the one we'd used at the Outlook farm, for a fifteen-year-old New Holland 907 fourteen-foot-wide, self-propelled, swather. The swather looked rough, but the motor was sound and the header was still in usable condition. With this equipment, I cut almost a thousand acres of our own and the neighbors' hay. The baling seemed to go on forever. The light hay was so dry it was only baleable with a dew on in the wee hours of the morning. Some mornings when the dew was light, we were able to bale only one or two hours at a time. As soon as the blazing summer sun inched over the horizon, the scant moisture disappeared. By seven o'clock a.m., the last of the dew was usually gone. When it got too dry, I had to quit baling or the puny hay crop would have been beaten to dust by the baler's plunger.

While I was harvesting the hay, my work day began at two-thirty a.m. After getting out of bed, I walked bare-footed in a sleep-shrouded trance out the porch door to the deck. With eyelids at half mast, I probed the fir planking beneath my bare feet for signs of dew. If the boards were bone dry, it was back to bed for a half-hour and then I got up and repeated the test. If my feet found dew, that was my wake-up call.

I soon found this method of dew checking inadequate. Conditions in the fields as far as six miles away from home were too different from those in the little canyon that sheltered our house and barns. The only way to determine if the hay was baleable out in the field was to get up and wait in the field for the dew, napping in the truck cab between dew checks. If the dew didn't come up by dawn, it wasn't going to and a good night's sleep was wasted for nothing. At first light, if there was no dew, I'd climb on another piece of equipment and start hauling bales or do more swathing. The days in the hay fields turned into weeks, and the weeks turned into months as we worked toward putting up the hay.

The grueling 1979 hay harvest ran from May 25 into July. I was out in our fields and saw the sun rise and set for forty-five days straight, my days starting in the predawn darkness at three a.m. with the tractor lights on and ended at ten o'clock at night, when it was too dark to see because I had no lights on my balewagon. I became a walking, work-worn zombie.

Sunday afternoon naps became my only relief from the demanding harvest schedule. I always headed to the back corner in the basement after Sunday lunch and slept straight through until baling time at three o'clock the next morning. For the first time in my life, my wellspring of energy and drive had been drawn to its limit, and it was running dry. I was becoming punch drunk, haggard, and increasingly depressed about our untenable situation on the Breaks Ranch as the baling progressed and the unavoidable numbers on the bale counter told our story. The year before the same acreage produced more than twice as much hay. We had another crop failure on our hands.

It made me heartsick to watch another whole year's work slip through my fingers. The fruits of our past successes in the valley were being drained rapidly by the Breaks Ranch. I thought about the hardships endured by the pioneers who opened this country, and I reflected on the history of the hard ranching country near our farm.

The number of settlers in the 1970s was far less than it was a hundred years earlier during the homesteading days. Back then, free land for the taking drew settlers into the unclaimed wilds opened by the Oregon Trail. However, the "free land" would have to be paid for in sweat and blood.

Smallpox from contact with whalers and fur traders decimated the native peoples before the time of Lewis and Clark, and the deadly flu and measles epidemics of the 1830s reduced the numbers of Indians even further from their former status as the largest native population in pre-Columbian North America.

The best lands along river bottoms were grabbed up in the 1850s, and the latecomers slowly spread out over what was left. Near the turn of the century, land promoters got the bright idea to plat a town site on the east end of was was now our Breaks Ranch. The town they envisioned would serve as the center for a new fruit-growing region, Horseshoe Bend. Reports had widely circulated back East about the fabulous fruit production the Inland Empire was capable of. However, regardless of the exaggerated claims of the promoters, Goldendale, due to its climate, was not to become a fruit-production center like the Yakima Valley, just a few miles north over the Simcoe Mountains.

The new town at Horseshoe Bend withered and died because of lack of a dependable water supply, hard winters, late-spring frosts, and generally poor soils for growing fruit trees. All that remained were small grain and cattle ranches, which were established before the land promoters moved in.

As I thought about the disappointments of the early settlers — the abandoned school, the empty church and cemetery, I couldn't help but connect our own perilous situation to the broken hopes of those who'd come before us. We were holding on with slipping fingers, and as the past clearly demonstrated, there were no miracles.

As I drove past abandoned homesteads that were now part of much larger farms, the thought kept haunting me: each of the windowless shacks had one day been just as new as the Monster house we were building. The conclusion was depressing and unavoidable.

On July 6, the mail was choked with the normal flood of bills. But among the letters was one from one of Ann's, former schoolmates which set in motion an idea upon which we pinned our hopes for financial salvation.

As I read over Helena James's letter after dinner, I said to myself, "A game about farming; that's not a bad idea." That was the idea put forth by Helena: creating a parlor game about agriculture that everybody would buy.

Ann nodded at my comment as she looked up from the sinkful of dishes. "Farming is such a gamble, it makes what people do at Reno and Las Vegas look penny ante."

"You've got that right!" I sighed.

While I brushed my teeth that night, I stared at the haggard, hay-worn figure that I saw in the mirror. I was more than thankful that I had only two or three mornings of hay baling left before I could start sleeping through the night again.

"A game about farming," I repeated, "not a bad idea at all."

7

The Game Invented
on the Seat of a
Tractor

• • • • • • • • • • • • • • • • • •

My alarm went off at three a.m. as usual, and I stumbled out of bed in a stupor, my mind still clutching at the last few shreds of slumber. I walked out the back door barefooted onto the deck. The soles of my feet were the only part of me that was fully awake, as they felt deck for signs of dew. The boards were bone dry. That meant that I could crawl back in bed for another half-hour of blessed but fitful sleep.

At three-forty-five, the dew came up. I dressed and headed out to the pickup truck with my breakfast, a peanut butter sandwich. If I was going to be up when any sane man would be sleeping, I might as well be in the field rather than hanging around the kitchen drinking coffee. I certainly didn't expect Ann to get up and make my breakfast in her thoroughly pregnant condition. She needed all the rest she could get. Besides, Ann also had full day of work ahead of her, pounding the pavement selling radio advertising. Based on the pace of our lives, a leisurely farm breakfast, complete with the table brimming with baked goods and cured meats seemed as distant in time as a Currier and Ives print.

The moon had set in the cloudless sky just after midnight. At four a.m., it was so dark and clear the night sky was ablaze with stars. The lights of Goldendale shimmered fifteen miles away like some earthbound constellation set in the sea of darkness below the brilliant horizon line. The ground beneath my feet looked dark and lifeless compared to the heavens with starlight radiating from a billion points above. I drove my pickup truck through the gate of the hayfield and parked next to my tractor. I had serviced the tractor and baler the day before so there would be no delay and I could get to baling immediately. No fumbling around in the dark trying to find the grease points on the baler driveline.

Baling at night, under tractor headlights, created an eerie feeling of isolation. It was a feeling of a ship at sea, impervious to the outside world, a self-contained capsule. Through the darkness the tractor pounded out its steady pulse of power. Inside a small tunnel of light the baler lapped up the ribbon of dry hay from the ocean of darkness. It was in those predawn hours that life seemed to be in harmony, as if the planet were fresh and unused, the problems and troubles of the world temporarily in abeyance. The world was mine for the taking, because in those wee hours I had it all to myself.

Slowly the eastern sky showed a few streaks of light. The sun, still below the skyline, ignited a wispy cloud hanging high above the desert, and it turned an incandescent orange. Running in the dark, straining to see shapes lurking at the edge of my envelope, required full concentration. I was relieved to see dawn come. With my tractor-sized world bathed in the brightness of a new day's light, I could now start to relax as I baled hay. I could start to toy with my many daydreams as the horizon glowed in the amber morning light. I started back to work on a novel I had been plotting for years in my mind, trying to pick up where I had left off the day before. I shuffled characters and scenarios in my head like so many file cards, trying to find the place I had left the story I was building.

All of a sudden an inspiration struck me like a bolt of lightning!

"This damn novel I'm working on makes a hell of a lot better board game than it does a book!" I yelled to myself above the din of the baler and tractor.

Apparently, my brain had churned all night on Helena's brilliant suggestion. The more I thought about it, the more sense it made.

One of the difficulties of my novel was the long span of time I needed to let my story unfold. As far as I was concerned, the story of farm life in America — the theme of my novel — could only be told properly when it was viewed across time. Farming, as we discovered, was predicated on years of planning and forethought in preparation for doing something years into the future. It was instantly obvious to me that the gaming track of our agriculture game should be the calendar year. That would allow the seasons to unfold, like real life, one after the other, as the game was played. Each trip around the game board would be one full year. Simple. My game now had a time line!

As the wispy clouds hung on the eastern skyline, they provided shade so the light dew on the ground held on long enough for me to bale until almost nine. Though my body operated the tractor, my mind was fully engaged somewhere else with details of the game.

One by one, all the things I had been trying to express with my novel were re-evaluated in a new format. It was obvious that the name of the board game had to be simple. I wanted a name that explained the product. A name that could be spelled or repeated on just one hearing. It seemed as obvious to me as the sun in the sky that the perfect name should be *The Farming Game*. It said it all. It was a name that easily could be remembered by anyone. *The Farming Game,* I thought to myself as I drove the pickup from the hayfield down the hill through the timber to our house.

The rest of the morning I spent repairing the guide wheel on the bale pickup of my New Holland 1045 balewagon. The day before, I hit a boulder that was hiding in the grass on the edge of the field and tore the wheel and bracket all to hell. Due to the mini-drought of '79, with the hay so light and the bales so far apart, I was running the balewagon a gear higher than normal. And, going too fast, I clipped the rock on a turn.

I finished my welding job at noon and went inside our empty house to make my lunch. Ideas about my boardgame buzzed around me like a swarm of bees all morning, making it difficult, almost hazardous, to get my farm work done. Over a sandwich and a glass of spring water I finally gave *The Farming Game* idea my full concentration.

There was absolutely no doubt about it now: my novel made a far better game than a book! My novel had been set in the diverse and fertile Yakima Valley, so why not do the same with the game? Perhaps I could put a map of the valley in the center of the board.

I went down to the basement and found a suitable scrap of sheetrock and a framing square. On the kitchen table I drew a game board. With the straightedge I laid out a gaming track, a square for each week of the year. The gaming track surrounded a map of the lower Yakima Valley. I divided the valley into irrigation districts, one for each of the six persons playing at being farmers. Every irrigation district had a house and set of outbuildings around which players could build their farms. I decided there would be several crops each game farmer could choose to diversify the outcome of the play. Harvesting would be spread around the calendar year just as it was in real life.

As I put my ideas down on paper, working feverishly at the kitchen table, a parlor game came to life. It was to be as straightforward as farming itself. A player would roll the dice to harvest, then consult the Harvest Rate Chart for the payoff amount. I thought rolling dice was just the right touch because in real life farmers had about as much control over harvest income as any gambler does. For the actual harvest payoff numbers, we'd use real-world figures, a blend of historic crop prices and yields.

Next, the player would draw an Operating Expense Card (before you get your harvest cash, you have to pay your bills). And, like all farmers, the player would be hoping that the crops brought in more cash than they cost to raise! The crops we'd use for the game would be Hay, Cattle, Grain and Fruit — crops raised in almost all fifty states.

Each player would start with a small farm he inherited from Granddad, and need a job in town to support himself. The starter farm wouldn't be big enough to make the family's living. Thus the necessity for the job in town. The object of the game would be to build the player's farm large enough for him to be able to quit his job, and come home to farm full time. If a player could do that without going broke, he'd win the game.

I never made it back outside to work that day. And by the time Ann and the boys came home that evening from working for the radio station, *The Farming Game* was fully hatched.

As I reviewed what I had created, I realized how closely I had converted real life on the farm to a schematic design true to the vagaries of farming. I remembered an article in a farm magazine earlier that week, which reported that in 1976, 45 percent of all the nation's two-and-a-half million farm families received more taxable income from their jobs in town than they did from their farms. The story of American farming was getting bigger. It was the direction in which the tide of agricultural history was running. Dr. Earl Butz, the Secretary of Agriculture, was instructing farmers that to survive they had to "get big or get out!" That concept was at the heart of *The Farming Game* which, if properly carried out, would be a faithful reproduction of actual challenges, disappointments and triumphs American farmers experienced, their crises included the duststorms, crop failures, fluctuating market prices, animal diseases, accidents, and weather disasters that plagued the men and women who worked to build a future out of the soil. There was no question that I had just invented a fantastic board game, and all afternoon I couldn't wait for Ann to come home so she could see the project that was going to be our salvation and our future.

Ann, worn from her Friday night thirty-five-mile commute with two hungry kids, was in no mood to hear about my newest hare-brained idea. The July day had been in the mid-nineties, and without air conditioning in the car, her ride home from work in The Dalles, with the boys screaming and fighting all the way, had been miserable. The combination of being four months pregnant, overheated, overtired, and downright cranky didn't put Ann in the best frame of mind to hear my scheme. She had gotten used to hearing my wild ideas, which came and went with the seasons, but *The Farming Game* idea was woolier than usual. However, I pitched my idea with such missionary fervor and in such detail that even Ann in her exhausted condition had to crack a smile.

The more I pitched the game idea to Ann, the more convinced I became that *The Farming Game* was the solution to our money troubles. Perhaps it was because Ann was as anxious as I to find a way out of our mess that she allowed herself to become convinced that the game was our pot of gold. We spent the weekend brainstorming about the fine details of the game. Ann went back to work on Monday; her doubts that trying to produce the game was like the compulsive gambler's last fling at the jackpot melting away. Perhaps it wasn't so crazy after all.

By the early part of that next week, I finished up the longest, most grueling hay harvest of my eight-year career in farming. Our puny, drought-strangled wheat crop was almost ready to thrash, and rather than pay to hire out the combining, we did what I had sworn I'd never do again: we bought a beat-up JD 55 level-land combine. It was twenty-five years old and still in fair running condition. With little effort I got it field-ready for harvest. Before we could start into the wheat, I also had to fix our battered grain-hauling truck. The transmission had finally turned to mush. The problem came as no surprise, since I had been nursing the truck along for almost two years with it popping in and out of gear. But now, no amount of pressure would hold it in gear any longer. There was absolutely no way that truck could haul a load of grain to the elevator without getting the transmission overhauled.

After much calling around, I found a repair shop in Portland, ninety miles away, which could rebuild my transmission, start to finish, in one day, provided I had the transmission in their shop by eight in the morning. Brother Kurt, who was now back out West and living in The Dalles, helped me pull the transmission. We put it in the back of my pickup truck for an early-morning cruise through the Columbia Gorge to the big city the following day.

Every spare moment in the intense week following inventing *The Farming Game* I devoted my time to fleshing out the smaller details of the game. I couldn't wait to get out on my tractor, away from the distractions of the house and shopwork, so I could concentrate as I drove in the fields. *The Farming Game* became the most amazing and all-consuming mental exercise I had ever experienced.

There were 175 days until Christmas, and I was aware that all big stores had completed most of their Christmas buying already. It followed that if we could get the game in production before the holidays, our main market would have to come from mail orders.

We thought about finding an established game company to produce *The Farming Game* but discarded the thought almost immediately. Time was short; the only way to get our game on the shelves by Christmas was to do it ourselves. It was doubtful in the few days left before Christmas, if a large company would even decide whether or not to buy our game, let alone produce it for the 1979 Holiday season.

I felt a driving sense of urgency to get *The Farming Game* on the market for Christmas 1979; there was no time to waste. If we waited a whole year, prudently searching for someone to produce my invention, our farm might be too far gone to save. I had a gut feeling that there was only the smallest window of time in which to make this game idea work. I was convinced that we had only one good shot to do this thing successfully. I felt very much like the pitcher who tries to throw a baseball through the window of a moving car — timing and aim were everything.

Another important consideration in proceeding with the idea ourselves was the simple fact that the person who puts up the money calls the shots and takes the profits. The producer, not the inventor, usually has the editorial control. Editorial control on this project was something I wasn't about to give up if I could help it. When I researched the business realities of bringing out our own boardgame, one thing was clear to me: we'd have to sell tens of thousands of games to generate enough profit to help with our farm-debt situation. If we had inherited the Breaks Ranch from Granddad, all paid for, with a few pieces of machinery thrown in, we probably could have made it through the tough times without too many problems.

But starting as we did, from scratch, we were carrying a crushing debt that was eating us alive. Four good years in Outlook had us cruising at full speed on the highway of success; two bad years out of three on the Breaks Ranch had let the air out of our tires, and we were now running on the rims.

After Kurt and I dropped off the truck transmission at the rebuild shop, we stopped at a cafe for breakfast. I picked up a copy of the Portland Yellow Pages and started to look up businesses I might need to get *The Farming Game* produced. If we were going to build thousands of games, we needed an assembly line and warehouse space, forklifts and loading docks. We also needed to find a box maker, a printer, and someone to produce the game board. I grabbed a handful of dimes, headed for the pay phone, and started dialing. The box company was the first thing I tried. In five or six calls I found two likely companies.

The idea occurred to me that assembling *The Farming Game* would make a perfect contract at a sheltered workshop. My sister was the activities director at Goodwill Industries in Portland, Maine, so Goodwill was the first place I thought of. There was a Goodwill Industries plant in Southeast Portland, Oregon. I called the number and was soon put in touch with their contracts officer. He said he would be glad to have me visit the plant and talk. He'd like to show me what Goodwill could do to help with my project. Working with Special-Ed kids part of the time during my year at the Yakima junior high gave me an appreciation for the productive capacity of the handicapped. I witnessed firsthand the pride and satisfaction they take in accomplishing a useful task.

My visit to the Goodwill plant was too good to be true. They had everything we needed in the way of equipment and facilities to assemble our game. Goodwill's protected workshop did a great range of assembly jobs as well as their traditional goods recycling. At the time, they didn't have enough assembly contracts to keep their client workers busy, so they were ready to bend over backwards to provide their services to us, including temporary free warehouse space. My next stop was to see a printer. There were five pages of printers listed in the Portland Yellow Pages, and several phone calls produced a list of places to visit. I searched in vain for a plastic molding company that could produce our game-playing pieces. Apparently nobody did that kind of work in the Portland area.

The grain truck's transmission was completed when we stopped to pick it up at four-thirty. On our drive back through the Gorge towards the ranch, the wheels in my head were spinning with possibilities. Though the idea of *The Farming Game* was born only the week before, I left

Portland convinced that if we got right after it, we could have our game out and ready to sell long before Christmas!

Many small and trivial details remained, such as financing, distribution, and finding the remaining manufacturers, but in the dream world Ann and I created at night, after the kids were in bed, it seemed possible. We had crossed the important first hurdle: we began to truly believe we could do it!

What we had to do next was to take the gamble. We decided immediately that we weren't going to mention *The Farming Game* to Ann's family. We knew from long experience that their first reaction would probably not be positive. It was obvious that if we asked anyone with real-world business experience, whether it was possible to make the game a financial success, the answer would be a resounding "NO!" So Ann and I pledged to each other not to talk about *The Farming Game* to her family until we had the game under production.

Helena and her husband, who provided us with the seed of the idea for *The Farming Game,* declined the opportunity to put up money and join us in manufacturing the game.

Ann and I knew our only course of action would be to mortgage whatever untapped real estate equity that was still available and sell a big part of our cattle herd to raise the money to manufacture the game. It was a momentous decision. Literally, we were betting the ranch that we would succeed. We never allowed ourselves to consider the other side of our future if our hopes, if the game, was a flop.

Ann came up with a brilliant solution to the technical problem of how to keep track of the cropland the gaming farmers bought while they played *The Farming Game.* Ann's suggestion was to use cling vinyl for acreage stamps.

A stamp represented a new field added to one's farm. It was a good idea, better than wooden or plastic markers that were easy to knock over.

Like 45 percent of all farmers, we'd been "weekend farmers," having to rely on Ann's jobs in town to make ends meet, and we hoped that the business of marketing *The Farming Game* would become our "job in town." We felt more legitimate when Ann went to the county courthouse and filed a DBA application (doing business as) under the name The Weekend Farmer Company. Now we had a product and a business entity which identified who we were.

As the second week after the invention of *The Farming Game* ended, the lineup of suppliers and components was progressing satisfactorily, and the more I thought about the idea of producing and marketing *The Farming Game* ourselves, the more I liked it. More than ever, I was absolutely sure I wanted total editorial and design control. The more I considered the alternative, of selling the idea to a big company, the more I felt it was wrong. I distrusted big corporations, and I knew that Ann and I had the gumption, the creativity, and the smarts to design and supervise the production of the game.

Even as plans for the game advanced, Kurt and I finished getting the wheat harvest equipment field-ready. We decided to take a three-day break and go over to the coast before the combining started. Our wheat was a little tough yet, not quite ready to harvest, and the haying was finally all done; it was high time for a break. We hopped in the car and drove to Seattle. As soon as we got to my mother-in-law's, I went to the phone book and within an hour had made an appointment with an attorney who specialized in copyright law.

I had already racked up a huge phone bill at home researching the problems of game production, finding out the how and the who of the game-publishing world. Our trip to see an attorney was the first upfront money we spent beyond our phone bills. We left our appointment with the lawyer authorizing him to spend money on a trademark search for the name we wanted to use: *The Farming Game.* The search would turn up anyone who had already laid claim to the name, or anything close to it. The trademark search was necessary for us to proceed farther. Anyone else using that name would cause terminal damage to our plans; the name was just perfect. A $350 review of the records in Washington, D.C., would show if *The Farming Game* was still an unbranded maverick.

When we returned home to the ranch I fired up the combine to cut our drought-stunted wheat crop. The first several rounds around the field confirmed my worst fears as to the yield of the crop. Another disaster. Round after depressing round on the combine, a grinding feeling of helplessness, kept pushing me down, repeating a refrain I already knew by heart: if we wanted to stay on this ranch, I had to do something dramatic, and soon. *The Farming Game* was the only thing I saw on our horizon with the potential to save us. But, oh God! What would happen to us if I were wrong?

Eighteen days after I invented the game, Ann and I made the joint decision that we were willing to bet the Breaks Ranch that we could make a success of *The Farming Game.* If desperation was the mother of invention, then we had pledged our future on a whim. Other people had gambled and won with much greater odds against them.

Since mail order seemed the logical way to get *The Farming Game* on the market its first year, all that was required to open a mail-order business was a post office box. So we went into town and rented one. I started calling magazine publishers for their rate cards and copy deadlines. I found that we had little time to prepare ad copy and submit it, as most of the national magazines needed ad copy by September 5 for their pre-Christmas issues.

I picked magazines that would reach people living in rural America and who might be interested in the subject matter of our game. We had twenty-three days to get our finished ad off to the publishers. Ann and I had stepped into an area where we obviously needed some professional help, and quick. We started looking for a graphic artist.

We were referred to Vern Groff, the owner of Studio Group in Portland, an advertising and graphics design firm. Vern had been raised on a small farm that was now under the Portland Airport and knew the Yakima area well. We hit it off immediately, and The Weekend Farmer Company commissioned a logo rendered from my design at Vern's shop. We would use the logo as the center of our magazine ad, and later put it on the box lid of the finished game.

We decided to run 10,000 copies as a first edition of *The Farming Game.* With the high set-up costs of the artwork, typesetting, the dies for the box manufacturer, and with the $1,000 I spent on phone calls, there was really no hope for making enough profit if we ran fewer than 10,000 games. If *The Farming Game* sold well, we dreamed we would eventually produce it in even larger runs to take advantage of the huge manufacturing savings, per unit, in printing.

Our rapid climb to our present precarious debt position had been, in great part, due to Ann's ability to work the numbers and present a loan-worthy image to the bank. Our borrowing philosophy for the first years we were farming was formed when inflation rates were higher than loan rates. Our plan was to borrow every cent we could get our hands on, and expand our operation as rapidly as possible. Somehow, Ann met every one of our loan payment deadlines for the hundreds of thousands of dollars we borrowed and paid back in the years we had been farming. Gene, our banker, tried his best to talk us out of the crazy idea of producing *The Farming Game*. It was too late; our minds were made up.

When Ann gave Les her two-weeks' notice at the radio station, he came unglued! She was his legs, ears and eyes down in the real world of The Dalles, while Les orbited the earth from his radio station hermitage high atop the mountain. I convinced her later to think of that unpleasant episode as a compliment, a recognition that she was a worthwhile employee, a pat on the back for a job well done. Ann promised Les to interview, hire and train a replacement for her position before she left.

As Ann drove down the switchback mountain road from the radio studio, two sparrow hawks played tag with her car as they flew from reflector to reflector down the windy track. The reflectors were an improvement that the Feds had made, so their maintenance man didn't drive off the road on his way up to the FAA beacon in the dense fog that could hang on the desert mountain the winter months of the year. The hawks flew ahead, hoping Ann's movement would scare up some prey. Near the bottom, the hawks left her to hunt the rock draw that cut at the mountain's base. A feeling of joy and release overcame her as she pulled up at the babysitter's. In two weeks she would be coming home, no matter how our new experiment worked out.

At best, we hoped to create a job for Ann at home that would not depend on grain or hay prices. At worst, we

would quit our insane rural adventure and I would search
for a career in the ivy-covered college cloisters before I was
too old to get retrained. Either way, after a long wait, Ann
was coming home to raise her babies.

8

Doing the Christmas Countdown

• • • • • • • • • • • • • • • • • • •

Our plan to bring *The Farming Game* to life in time for Christmas season hinged on having a printer that we could count on. After the boxing and a few plastic parts, our game was primarily made of printed paper. After shopping around we decided the printing would be done in Portland at the giant printer, Graphic Arts Center. Graphic Arts had every size and configuration of printing press, from the smallest all the way up to the monster web presses, taking paper by the two-ton roll in one end and spitting stapled, folded and pre-addressed catalogs out the other end. Graphic Arts ran three shifts, seven days a week, at a level of efficiency and punctuality that would make the military jealous. There was even a typesetting and litho-prep operation in-house. The printer assured us that they would be more than able to meet any production schedule or size that we could throw at them. To start the ball rolling, our account executive said we needed to pay one-third of the total cost of the print job immediately, if we wanted to schedule the press time needed to meet the tight time demands of our project.

The game board was to be manufactured by a company in Los Angeles. Game boards are constructed from two sheets of recycled paperboard taped together like a hinge, and then the whole thing is back-wrapped with the customary black textured paper. The last production step was to laminate our face label onto the unwrapped side on the game board. Our deposit secured the schedule to have the face labels printed at Graphic Arts on September 10. They would be shipped down to Los Angeles for lamination. The game board company would then ship the finished boards to Goodwill back in Portland, for placement into the finished product.

The game box, interior money tray, and platform could all be made in Portland, we discovered. We contracted with Grigsby Brothers Paper Box Company, which assured me they could meet our time requirements without any problem. All we had to do was provide them the final art and a third of the money up front with our production order.

After much searching we finally found Engrave Inc., a plastic molding company in Ohio. We had found lots of plastics molders, but finding one who agreed to manufacture the small run of our playing markers for *The Farming Game* — a miniature farmer decked out in coveralls and a straw hat — was difficult.

There had been no problem in locating dice. Ann found half-a-dozen sources for dice in her research in the library in The Dalles. The Thomas Register of Manufacturers, on file there, had proved invaluable in our search for components.

I put my dialing finger to work following up the leads she found in the library. If the company I reached didn't do the type of work I was seeking, I asked for a reference to a company that did, and kept on asking until I found all the companies I needed. The phone bill chasing these leads for all our components grew to $1,500. A big phone bill is part of the cost of doing business from the middle of nowhere.

The day the game was invented, I drew a sketch of the logo that we would use on the box lid. We needed that same design for our magazine display ads with fast-approaching copy deadlines. So creation of *The Farming Game* logo was the first project for our graphic designer.

The logo I'd envisioned contained all the elements of our game. Surrounding the miniature farmer, standing happy and confident center stage, was his cartoon farm world. A cow, an apple tree, a bale of hay, a sheaf of wheat. A stormcloud threatened in the background. Vern, our designer, liked my composition the minute he saw it. After three or four days, Vern had me come back to Portland to see what he had created using my ideas.

The design of the logo was the same yet marvelously different. Vern had done a super job of bringing my ideas to life. The scene was just exactly as I had specified; the only substantive difference was that Vern had added a nice touch: a hoe in the hand of my farmer, a la *American Gothic*. Vern himself had once used a long-handled hoe to weed the family five-acre spud patch, summer after summer as a kid. The experience had convinced him that he didn't want to spend the rest of his life doing manual labor. He couldn't resist putting his old nemesis to work in the logo. I liked it; the hoe stayed.

Then we were set back on our heels by a call from our copyright attorney in Seattle. He advised us that his trademark search had turned up no reason we could not use *The Farming Game* trademark. His search, however, had turned up many trademark registrations for other games

about farming, stretching back to 1950. I was dumb-
founded. I had expected the search to turn up maybe two or
three, but his search had uncovered almost twenty farming
games, all of which had slid into obscurity. I was face to
face with a real body count of agriculture games that hadn't
made it. I admit I was shocked, but neither Ann nor I
allowed this reality check to change our minds. Besides, it
was too late. We were already committed. We bowed our
necks and charged straight ahead. We were convinced that
we had built a better mousetrap, and America would eventually beat a path to our door.

We mailed our magazine ads with checks totaling more
than $12,000 to pay for ad space in four national magazines.

The expenses of building our game seemed to rise each
week. Graphic Arts Center's final bid on printing our cards,
bank notes, and money was several thousand dollars above
the first estimates. Looking for ways to trim production
expenses, Ann determined that if we bought our own paper
cutter, collated and cut all the cards that went into *The
Farming Game,* we could save about $3,000 in labor
charges at the printers. So for $750 we bought a manual
paper cutter to do the job. I was going to be Manuel on the
handle, slicing tons of paper, two-and-a-half inches at a
time.

The game cards were printed right on schedule; the
first completed run was finished late Saturday night the first
week in September. The next day, on his day off, the superintendent of the typesetting and small press shop at Graphic
Arts, put three-quarters of a ton of freshly printed cards in a
company delivery van and, with his wife, drove them up the
Columbia Gorge from Portland. We were grateful. Though
Graphic Arts was by far the largest printer on the West
Coast, they gave us friendly, down-home treatment. It was a

great boost working with industry professionals who were so obviously rooting for us to succeed. And even more important, it was grand to work with a company that delivered on time every single one of the dozen jobs related to *The Farming Game.*

While keeping our project moving forward, I was commuting three or four days a week the 180 miles from the ranch to Portland and back. In the complicated process of getting *The Farming Game* built, there was no substitute for riding herd on the operation in person. The almost-daily drive through the Columbia River Gorge let me witness summer turning into fall as I watched the mosses spring to life again on the basalt cliffs with the coming of the autumn rains. Early frosts had nipped the oaks and turned them orange up at the ranch, but in the lower elevations of the Klickitat Canyon and along the mighty Columbia River, the leaves of the cottonwoods and alders and oaks were still dark green; they had yet to show signs that summer had really passed.

Days I did not spend on the big-city commute I sat on horseback gathering our cows off the High Prairie range. It was time to sell half our herd of cattle. We needed cash to cover the checks that Ann was writing almost daily. The real costs of getting our game together were getting dangerously higher than our estimates. Raising the money for our game venture was by far the greatest act of creative banking that Ann ever attempted.

On the afternoon of September 15, we got a call from our screen printers. The vinyl we needed for the game coming from Colorforms had just arrived by motor freight. "But where," the printer asked, "was the cardboard backing the vinyl was supposed to be clinging to?" Without backing, the vinyl was as soft and pliable as warm saltwater taffy. "There is no way we can print on the stuff the way it is," he said.

As I hung up the phone, my stomach tightened with tension. What had gone wrong?

By leaving the ranch at six a.m., I was in Portland at eight o'clock for the start of business the next morning. Sure as can be, there was no cardboard backing! The sheets of vinyl, each the size of a large bath towel, were stacked on five oversized pallets with a layer of tissue paper between each sheet, like massive slices of cheese from the deli counter. The owner of the screen print shop picked up a sheet of the vinyl by its corners, and it hung from his hands like freshly thrown pizza dough. The printer was adamant: there was no way he would even waste his time trying to work with the vinyl without the backing. No way.

I phoned back East immediately from the print shop office and was told that if I had wanted the slick cardboard backing, I should have asked for it.

While we waited for the vinyl backing from the East, we were busy at home with collated colored paper stacked everywhere. Farmers Fate Cards, Option to Buy Cards, and Operating Expense Cards, along with three denominations of bank notes and five denominations of money, made a two-ton pile in the living room. My mother, who had recently moved west, helped us collate the cards quilting-bee style to ready them for our puny, muscle-powered paper cutter.

The progress we were making down in the basement on the cutter was slow but steady. I had calculated that, when we were done, Ann and I would have cut and rubber-banded about 1,500,000 pieces of paper the size of a business card. I didn't have the nerve to figure out how many hours the job was going to take us. Common sense told me it was so many hours, I didn't want to know.

We had shipped the limp, unbacked vinyl over to Goodwill, and when the backing finally arrived from Colorforms, we set about finding a method of putting the two pieces together. The screen printers needed the vinyl to be smooth and wrinkle free, firmly stuck to its backing, before they could print on it. The clients at Goodwill did their best laying the stretchy vinyl sheets down on the backing. Since air bubbles trapped underneath the vinyl needed to be eliminated, we tried hand-held ink rollers. The job was frustratingly slow. But worse, when we took a sample over to the screen printers, we found that this technique was inadequate. Pressure from the squeegee pushing the ink through the printing screen also bunched up the little tiny air bubbles between the vinyl and the backing and made an unusable mess of the final printed product.

My heart sank. We tried printing over and over, with the same results, until we had used up all the samples I'd brought from Goodwill. We had not printed a single usable copy. The vinyl acreage-stamp component was a complete disaster. I drove home through the Columbia Gorge with this problem stewing in my guts, half afraid I had just witnessed the beginning of the end. It seemed that he uncharted swamp of toy manufacturing was starting to suck us under.

While I was in the city, our cows had broken through a fence and were in Earl and Helen's field to the east of us. Ann said Helen was mad enough to call twice to find out when I was going to show up and get our damn cows out.

After changing out of my city clothes, I saddled up my big red horse and rode over to get our pasture poachers. In my ride along the border fence through the woods and across the alfalfa fields I found a section the cows had obliterated. The hole was big enough for every cow and calf in the bunch to slip through the breech. Surveying the damage, I knew that I had an hour of fence fixing ahead of me that evening, after I chased the cows home. With the pasture so short, due to the mini-drought, it was hard to keep our cows in. They knew that there must be better grass somewhere else than the skimpy feed we'd provided in front of them; and if a rickety fifty-year-old fence was all that stood in their way, they would just go right through it. By the time I repaired the gaping hole, the sun was long down. I finished the job by the headlights of the pickup truck. All that evening the problems with the vinyl kept circling me like vultures. I was dead tired and as depressed as I had ever been in my entire life when I arrived home.

The next day, after doing my morning chores in the predawn light, I left for another two-hour drive into Portland. The rays of morning sun filled the Gorge with brilliance as they danced on the waters of the broad Columbia and illuminated to glowing the surrounding basalt cliffs. I was struck by the bareness of Mount Hood looming behind the town of Hood River as I crossed the toll bridge to reach the interstate highway on the Oregon shore. Drought continued to grip the Northwest, but the mighty Columbia, turned into a series of unchanging lakes by the hydroelectric dams, seemed impervious to the dry conditions.

During the night, some brilliant person at the screen print shop had come up with the idea of using a cabinet shop's formica lamination setup to roll out the remaining air bubbles between the vinyl and its backing. In the morning, they borrowed one from a neighboring business and set it up in the screen print shop. It worked like a charm, and soon my bubble problem was history.

The whole mess with the vinyl probably happened because I had been trying to cut back on my telephone calls.

I saved $5 on one last call I chose not to make to Colorforms a few days before our vinyl was shipped. I had been planning to phone and chat and make sure everything was all straightened out with our order. But instead I decided to save a few bucks on a call I thought was probably a waste of time. It had occurred to me that we never discussed the slick cardboard backing, but like an idiot, I assumed they came together. The $5 savings eventually ended up costing us $2,500 and countless new grey hairs.

When the screen printers got through the mountain of backed vinyl, it was shipped to Grigsby Brothers, our box manufacturer. They had already started delivering the box tops, bottoms and seven-compartment money trays to Goodwill. They had also prepared a die to cut out the vinyl acreage stamps. I watched with intense interest as Walt, the owner, handled the first sample of vinyl coming off the die press. As I saw a second and third sample come off the press just the way they were supposed to, a flush of relief went through me as I realized the vinyl problem was now behind us.

Back at the ranch, Ann, in her eighth month of pregnancy, was larger than she'd been with her prior pregnancies. She and I spent many weary, repetitive hours on the paper cutter in the basement. Little by little, we whittled away at the tons of paper around us, upon which play money, cards and bank notes for the game were printed. By the first of October, Ann and I had cut enough of each variety of the cards that Goodwill could start assembly of the game just as soon as the last of our other parts came in. We still had countless hours more to be put in on the cutter, but we were making visible headway. Blake and Davey, our interested toddlers, helped in the way only little boys could. We counted toes and fingers every night to make sure none had been lost.

Ann was getting so big with our baby that she was having trouble getting close enough to the paper cutter to handle the paper stacks. One morning, while slicing through a stack of bank notes for the umpteenth time, I looked down at my pregnant partner handling the paper as it came off the knife. A tidal wave of affection broke over me. I was convinced as never before that I'd married the most perfect woman in the world.

By October 15, right on schedule, we had all the components gathered at Goodwill that we needed to start assembly, except for one: the game boards. Finishing all the cards and money would probably take another month or two of slaving in the basement at the rate we were going, but we had enough cut that we could assemble the first 5,000 games. I was feeling great! We had practically killed ourselves, but we had almost made it. Now, the only component missing was our game boards, which were due in at Goodwill any day. With the boards, we would finally have product to show store buyers with just enough time to spare to fill their Christmas orders.

One chain of stores was showing some interest in stocking our game. This was Western Farmers Co-op, with fifty outlets in rural Washington. There was a Western Farmers store in Goldendale, and the manager had taken a liking to me and the game idea. He had called the co-op's buyer in Seattle and made an appointment for me. I was to show *The Farming Game* to their new product-buying committee, which was in the process of making the final purchasing decisions for the winter season.

In early October I called Phil Spuler, the reporter from the *Yakima Herald* who ran the beautiful, full-page color story on Ann and the triticale baked goods when we lived on the farm in Outlook. Phil told me she thought our new adventure sounded interesting and invited me to Yakima to show her how *The Farming Game* worked.

Rather than wait until the game boards arrived, the next day I took all the parts I had, including a litho-sheet face label like those being laminated on boards in Los Angeles, and drove to Yakima to see Phil. I felt genuine excitement about *The Farming Game's* ability to tell the story of the American farmer and the unpredictability of rural life. With the farm crisis brewing on the national horizon in 1979, it seemed vital that farmers use every means possible of telling our cousins in town about just what went on beyond the blacktop. *The Farming Game* could also provide farm families a way to laugh at some of the disasters that befell them in real life. The enthusiasm I displayed while giving my sales pitch was infectious, and by the time I left the Yakima paper, I was feeling sure that they would print some kind of an article about our game.

Ann and I traveled to Seattle to make our presentation to the Western Farmers buying committee. The head buyer was mildly enthusiastic about *The Farming Game* during our presentation, but we met with almost stony indifference from the rest of the committee, the store managers. Western Farmers sold feed, seed, fertilizer, fuel, and farm supplies, not toys. The fact that we had been members of the co-op for six years was enough to get our product a polite hearing, but we left the meeting feeling doubtful of our chances of getting the game on the shelf in our own farm co-op.

The head buyer, Deloris, called late Friday afternoon to tell us that the decision, whether or not to add *The Farming Game* to the Western Farmers product line, had been deferred until Monday. She promised she would call us as soon as she knew, one way or the other, after the weekend.

On Sunday on the front page of the family living section of the *Yakima Herald* appeared a full-page story about *The Farming Game!* The story was illustrated with a big cartoon farmer playing our game by the staff artist. The cartoon more than made up for the absence of a finished product to photograph. We learned that the story was picked up by the Associated Press wire and played in most of the papers in the Northwest the same day!

Deloris from Western Farmers called excitedly on Monday morning. *The Farming Game* story, which ran in the *Seattle Post Intelligencer* over the weekend, had pushed the buying committee over the edge. Western Farmers was going to carry our game! Not only that, but she gave me a purchase order over the phone for 600 games ASAP. We were on our way! We had our very first order, almost $6,000 worth. All we had left to do now was get the damn game boards in at Goodwill so we could start assembling our product.

The November issues of the magazines running our ads, hit the stands in mid-October. Checks and orders came flooding into our post office box within the following week.

Just when things were looking up, delivery of our game boards was now more than a week late. Everything at Goodwill was set up and waiting for assembly, but without the game boards the whole operation was on hold. I finally got antsy and called the game board company in Los Angeles. I was connected with their salesman who I had met with in September in Portland. I said I was calling for bill of lading information so I could start a tracer on the shipment of my game boards, which I assumed were hung up somewhere. There was a long pause.

"Wait just a minute," he said. "Let me go check the paperwork on that," and then he put me on hold.

I hung on. Finally he came back on the line and sheep-ishly said, "Your game boards haven't been run yet."

"What!" I bolted out of my seat, my blood pressure shooting to a cuff-popping high. "What do you mean, they haven't run yet? Those game boards were supposed to have been in Portland a week ago!"

"Well," he said lamely, "we've had a machine breakdown, and we are behind on production."

"Is it fixed? When are my boards going to run? I need them pronto!" I gulped.

"It will be a couple of days," he answered. "I've got a call on another line, so I'll have to go," and the line went dead.

"Yeah," I said into the dead receiver, "like horse puckey you've got a call on the other line, you @$#%*&# weasel."

I was furious, frustrated and worried. Orders were piling up. Our whole project had hit another massive snag. We couldn't put the lid on a single box until we had all the parts that went inside. "Get a hold on yourself," I admon ished. "We still have plenty of time till Christmas," I thought. "Don't panic." We couldn't have made it this far merely to allow ourselves to be derailed by Horse Puckey, the name I'd given the game board salesman. "Besides," I told myself, "he assured me that our boards would be run in the next few days."

I waited five more days and called Horse Puckey back to check on the progress. He said all his machinery was up and running. There was a two-and-a-half-day job on the laminator, and when it was finished, *The Farming Game* was next in line.

Three days later I called Horse Puckey again for a status report. He was out, and the secretary said he was checked out for the rest of the day. I gave her my number and asked that he return my call as soon as he got back in.

Meanwhile the business calls we'd made had reached critical mass on our rural, four-party phone line. I had used our rotary-dial phone so much since I had invented *The Farming Game* that I developed a large and crusty callus on the inside of my index finger. Telephone service was essential for us to do business from the country, and we had gotten so busy that the neighbors who shared the line started to complain. The only alternative was for us to get a private line installed, even though the monthly charge was going to be outrageous. Figured at a rate of seventy-five cents per month for every quarter-mile from town, it was going to cost us $45 per month just for basic service.

On Wednesday the first call I placed on our new private line was to Horse Puckey, the game board salesman, who had failed to return my previous day's call. When I reached him, he reported that the game boards were scheduled to be run on Thursday and Friday, and he'd give me a call the minute they were on a truck headed to Portland.

Horse Puckey didn't call. Another week slipped by with no game boards.

While I should have been riding Horse Puckey to get our game boards off his production schedule and into my hands, I was busy gathering the last of our cattle which had strayed from our range in search of new feed and were scattered all over the north side of The Dalles Mountain. To cover our feed shortage I had rented forty acres of third-cutting irrigated meadow hay. The hay had been left standing for our cows to pasture off in the field. I gathered the cows with the invaluable help of Ann's youngest sister, Barb. After we corralled a load, we hauled them across the valley to the rented pasture.

To haul the animals, we had only the three-quarter-ton pickup with stock racks and a one-ton horse truck capable of hauling no more than five cows at a time. Rounding up and hauling our cows and their feedlot-sized calves the twenty-five miles to the new pasture, a few at a time, took all of my attention for days. Whenever I could, I played phone tag with the elusive Mr. Horse Puckey.

In her state of advanced pregnancy, Ann was worthless as a cowboy. Besides Ann had her hands full with *The Farming Game* business, which was getting busier all the time. We were both getting more frustrated and angry as the piles of paid orders from the magazine ads grew larger, and without the game boards we were unable to ship. We were both elated with the orders that came in, confirming the game's potential popularity, and furious at the salesman who had consistently lied to us.

As the first week in November ended, Horse Puckey's promises of delivery of our game boards grew more vague. The people at Goodwill had bagged all our dice and markers and worked through mountains of vinyl, bagging individual sets. They had also set up the thousands of game boxes and trays, ready to start the production.

I spent a great deal of time at Goodwill troubleshooting the various tasks we had created for them. I was extremely pleased with their dedication to our job. Our association with them was such a positive experience, we printed "Assembled at Goodwill" on the side panel of the box as a way of confirming our high regard.

Monday of the second week of November, I got Horse Puckey on the line again. I asked him where my game boards were. His answer slithered out, and I sensed before he finished hedging, even though he promised the boards would be run two days later, that I was getting another runaround. I had a signed bid from him with a delivery schedule, a delivery time that had long since lapsed. The contract was only a hollow promise until we had our game boards in hand. Of course, I could sue for noncompliance, but that wouldn't help us for the present.

One thing was abundantly clear to me: if we didn't get the game boards soon, we were going to miss the Christmas selling season entirely, and those consequences I did not wish to contemplate — nothing short of complete financial ruin.

I came to a decision. I was going down to L.A. to see for myself on the very next day.

With the new excuses ringing in my ears from Horse Puckey, I called for a plane reservation to Los Angeles for the following morning. I booked a flight out of Portland at seven a.m. and arrived in L.A. at ten. My only baggage was a copy of the morning newspaper. I wore my one-and-only business suit for my unannounced descent on the game board manufacturer.

By ten thirty-five, my cab from the Los Angeles Airport lurched across a railroad track and into the large, asphalt-covered yard in front of a huge, rusting World War Two vintage hangar-sized building. The name on the building matched the one on Puckey's business card. The cab fare was $30, and I paid it with haste.

I could almost smell my prey among the industrial odors that accosted my country-rarefied nose. The hunt was closing and my pulse quickened. I entered the building through the open bay doors and asked the first workman I saw where the office was. He pointed across the whirring machinery at a second-story cubicle against the far wall of the hangar. I picked my way down the yellow-painted foot lanes on the concrete floor to the office that sat perched inside the giant hangar like a tree fort. At the foot of the stairs to the office, there was a storage area with dozens of pallets of various kinds of printed materials.

My eye caught sight of a familiar design. What I saw was my own pallet of game board face labels, all nice and tidily shrink-wrapped in its plastic cocoon just as it had been shipped from Graphic Arts Center in Portland a month and a half earlier. An accumulation of production floor dust muted the bright colors of the face labels. That sight gave me a full head of steam, and I bustled up the stairs to the office, opened the door, and walked in. Across half-a-dozen desks I spied Horse Puckey. He was standing talking to an older, well-dressed man. I assumed the second person must be the plant manager, who I had talked to once or twice when I couldn't reach Horse Puckey himself.

I made a beeline across the sea of office furniture in Puckey's direction. His back was to me as I made my advance. At about ten feet and closing, Puckey turned to see who was coming up on his blind side. At four feet away, I stuck out my hand in the universal greeting of business the world over. I could see the puzzled expression on my quarry's face; it was obvious that he did not yet recognize me. Puckey's hand went out by reflex, as if I had struck the right spot on his elbow with a doctor's little rubber hammer. He was mine. As I towered over him, made even taller with the two-inch heels on my cowboy boots, he grabbed my outstretched hand. I put my full hay-bale-bucking 230 pounds into my grip.

Puckey's face went flush as I said, "George Rohrbacher, *The Farming Game.* I've come to see about my game boards."

I had him by complete surprise, and when I let go of his hand, he blanched as he looked down to see if all the fingers were still attached. I now had Horse Puckey's full and complete attention.

He hastily concluded his business with the plant manager, and when he took me on the obligatory plant tour downstairs, it was obvious that he was shaken. I let him do all the talking, only responding tersely with yes or no when he directly asked a question. When we finished the tour, Horse Puckey asked if he could take me out to lunch, even though it was just a few minutes past eleven o'clock. I said that sounded fine, as my airline breakfast had long since burned away in the chase.

Lunch was at a Japanese restaurant with knives and meat cleavers clanging, one of those restaurants where the meal is cooked practically in your lap. After his third rum and Coke, it came out that Horse Puckey had underbid our job by 40 percent because he hadn't taken into account that *The Farming Game* game board was much bigger than standard size. His company would lose money on the job, and management was hoping that if they just stalled us, we would miss the Christmas season, go broke, and just dry up and blow away.

On Puckey's dinner plate I laid a Xerox copy of the contract bid he signed and sent to us months ago before we dove headlong into this bet-the-ranch adventure. I explained gruffly that every nickel we had in the world was riding on this gamble. I explained that I had a pregnant wife and two baby boys that would be thrown out into the street when we lost our farm. I let him know in no uncertain terms that I held him personally responsible! I was willing to go to any ends to pursue him personally, if the contract to produce our game boards wasn't honored, and right away! He could not have missed the threat in my voice, or of the possibility of my intention to do him harm.

Horse Puckey probably viewed me as dangerous, a man ready to crack. Well, he was right. Five days later, we received the first shipment of game boards at Goodwill in Portland.

On Monday of Thanksgiving week we had all the components and were ready to assemble!

9

Paydirt

· · · · · · · · · · · · · · · · ·

November brought biting weather — snow flurries and deep, cold, freezing nights to the Breaks Ranch. The first snow of major consequence hit Thanksgiving Day.

Fully loaded with hay for the cows, I drove the pickup to a field a mile and a half up the hill from our hay barn. Ponderosa pines hanging heavy with snow closely lined the roadway. All was still except for the sound of my four-wheel drive plowing through the freshly fallen foot of snow.

The snow swirled in a blinding curtain as the truck pulled up to the gate into the pasture where we fed. The falling snow pelted me in the face through the half-opened window. Once in the field, I put the transfer case in four low and the automatic transmission into first gear, and I turned over the wheel of the truck to my five-year-old son Blake. I hopped on the back of the slowly moving pickup truck and began to feed off the hay. The blizzard's morning light was dull, and the visibility was so poor that I could see only about half of the herd as they charged at the truck trying to be first to the alfalfa.

The cows seemed extra happy to see me that Thanksgiving morning, though it probably had nothing to do with the holiday. The cows soon lagged behind the truck and tore at the hay sections in the snow. The sections of hay, as they fell from the truck, disappeared almost completely in the light powder. Blake, being big for his age, was just able to see over the dashboard and step on the gas pedal at the same time while clinging to the steering wheel. The truck slowly plowed on across the field, the cows trailing behind, bawling as they fought for the feed. When I finished dropping the hay, Blake and I drove slowly back through the cows to watch them eat and check them for any problems that might need treating.

As we finished feeding, the familiar voice of Paul Harvey came on over the truck radio with his noon report. Being Thanksgiving Day, he had a special newscast in store for us. Paul Harvey delivered the most rousing pro-American, apple pie, motherhood, and free-enterprise sermon I ever heard. His glowing pride in America truly moved me. During much of his talk, I felt he was speaking directly to what Ann and I were striving to do with our farm, with our game, with our lives. Sitting in my truck with my firstborn son looking out the window at our cows through the falling snow, I had the deepest rush of patriotism that I'd ever experienced for America, the land of golden opportunity.

Goodwill was finally going to start the full assembly of our game on Monday after the Thanksgiving holiday.

That busy world in Portland seemed as far away as the moon from where I sat Thanksgiving Day watching the cows eat. Observing the cows picking the hay out of the snow, it struck me that Paul Harvey might understand what

The Winter's Hay

I was trying to do and help spread the word. I had already planned to send the first two copies of our game to President Jimmy Carter and Secretary of Agriculture Bergland, so I might as well send Paul Harvey the third copy! The prospects of having our first game headed for the White House had the assembly floor of Goodwill all a-titter with excitement as full assembly was about to commence.

Everyone at Goodwill saw the logic of sending our farmer President, Peanut Jimmy, a *Farming Game.* Their name was proudly on the side panel of the box: Assembled at Goodwill Industries. This meant that they were going to the White House, too. It gave me enormous satisfaction to be involved with the special people at Goodwill. Work was a tonic for their ills or deficiencies.

Stu, the contracts officer at Goodwill, and I decided the first *Farming Game* down the assembly line needed some kind of send-off ceremony. I ordered a sheet cake and some balloons. Ann handed out sweatshirts printed with *The Farming Game* logo. We took lots of pictures, and the president of Goodwill of Oregon and I each wrote letters to the President to explain our gift of *The Farming Game.* With the game we included a copy of the full-page *Yakima Herald* article as additional explanation of where the gift was coming from. My letter read:

November 26, 1979

Dear President Carter:

The Farming Game *accompanying this letter is a present to you and your family from the Rohrbacher family. It is the first copy of our game to come off the assembly line at Goodwill Industries, Portland, Oregon.*

The past two winters farmers from all across the nation have gone to Washington, D.C., to express themselves. They want to be heard by you, the Congress, and the American people. We farmers feel that most of those in this country who eat have lost touch with just what it takes to grow their breakfast, lunch, and dinner.

This century as people abandoned farming by the millions for more remunerative occupations, they began to not need to plan much beyond their next month's paycheck, or have any more invested in their "meal ticket" than a lunchbox and a coffee cup. The vagaries of weather, markets, embargo, and pestilence faded from public experience, becoming far away and manageable. The corner grocery store has never yet run out, so your average American assumes it never will. The object of The Farming Game *is the object of half of our nation's farmers; you start with a couple of acres and a job in town to support it. Now, try to build that place into a full-time outfit that supports you.*

This is my effort to shed some light and spread some humor.

Yours respectfully,
George Rohrbacher

When the UPS truck hauled away the two copies for Washington, D.C., and the copy to Paul Harvey in Chicago, I breathed a sigh of relief. We were finally under way. The months of nonstop work and agony were about to bear fruit.

I wrote a short press release like the ones I once saw come across the desk at Les's radio station. I sent the press

release and my President Carter letter off to all the newspapers in the area the next day. *The Dalles Chronicle* ran a
story immediately. The editor loved my game idea, and his
story about it was placed on his paper's wire service.

Our weekly hometown paper, *The Goldendale
Sentinel,* still hadn't done an article on our game. Two
months earlier in September, at the county fair, the editor
walked past our display advertising, in three-foot-high
letters, the world premiere of *The Farming Game* without
stopping. There was no coverage in my own backyard. I
finally decided to drop off a copy of our press release and
then wait and see if the *Sentinel* could sniff out the story
from there.

Agriculture, as a topic, was prominent in the national
news with the tractorcades the past two winters. The
national media was looking for unique ways to report the
goings-on in rural America and thought our efforts with *The
Farming Game* newsworthy. We were bringing *The
Farming Game* to the market for many reasons, our
economic survival being only one. Many people in agriculture felt it was long past time for farmers to speak out and
put our case before the public.

In the early seventies, for the first time in a generation,
farmers experienced enough good years in a row to really
benefit from the American Economic Miracle which had
been blessing most other sectors of the economy since the
end of World War Two. When the Economic Miracle evap-
orated in the late seventies and became a full-blown
Agricultural Depression, the tractorcades started as farmers
hit the streets to press their case. *The Farming Game* was
the way I had found to speak out.

Five days after we sent the first game to President
Carter, Paul Harvey's characteristic greeting, "Hello

Americans!" preceded his full report on *The Farming Game*. All hell broke loose that afternoon at the Weekend Farmer Company! Our phone rang off the hook for days afterward. We got a number of calls from other reporters and from retailers who were being hounded by their customers and wanted to carry our game in their stores.

If we only could have had *The Farming Game* on store shelves nationwide at that moment when people went out looking for it after Paul Harvey's broadcast, who knows how many copies we could have sold! As it was, our games were flying off the shelves everywhere they were available. Western Farmers Co-op was selling our game like hotcakes. No sooner had our first order been delivered than all the games were snapped up by customers. The friendly buyer, Deloris, called and more than doubled her previous order. She said her managers were screaming for *The Farming Game*. She begged me to deliver a load of games to their Goldendale branch two days later on Saturday morning. She arranged a trucking network so the games would be distributed throughout the Western Farmers Co-op system over the weekend. If our games were shipped to their main warehouse in Tacoma, the normal distribution system would take ten days to disperse them. Our product was hot. Demand was so strong that they couldn't keep *The Farming Game* on the shelves! The former skeptics were now ordering by the truckload.

On Friday I drove down to Portland in my one-ton horse truck, which I shoveled clean for the occasion. I picked up every finished game on hand at Goodwill to be hauled to the ranch. The production line at Goodwill was operating at full capacity, and we were selling *Farming Games* quicker than we could produce them. Our mail-order business was buzzing, and store orders were pouring in as the Christmas selling season got into full swing. I unloaded one-third of the truckload of *The Farming Game* at home, resupplying the inventory in our living room. The rest of the games were delivered into the waiting arms of three out-of-town Western Farmers store managers on a supply run for their individual districts. Due to free-enterprise initiative, on Monday morning every one of the fifty stores in the co-op chain had a fresh supply of *The Farming Game* on hand to meet the Christmas rush.

Ann and I were exhausted. We had been running nonstop for the four months and one week that elapsed since the day I came up with the game idea. We had made myriad deadlines by the skin of our teeth, any one of which could have kept us from getting the game in the box for the Christmas season. We had pushed and we had shoved, we had burned the midnight oil, but we had gotten the job done.

Our third gestating child was now almost two weeks overdue. Our full concentration had been on bringing my cardboard baby into the world and getting it up and going. And, to our great joy, *The Farming Game* was taking off like a rocket! The word of mouth spread like wildfire: *The Farming Game* was a kick in the pants, fun as all get-out; it was one heck of a good time! When I returned from my delivery to Western Farmers Saturday afternoon, I was glowing. The store managers who came to pick up their games told me they thought *The Farming Game* was the hottest thing since Velcro! Proud father that I was, I believed them.

When I returned from town, Ann was working fever- ishly to finish the day's mail order. The boys played hide- and-seek in the piles of games and cardboard mailers that were stacked by the ton in our unfinished, warehouse-sized living room. Ann looked up at me from amid the clutter; she had a siren smile on her face. She grabbed both my hands and pulled me to her. Looking deep into my eyes, she told me our baby was coming.

Laura was born at home on the ranch with a doctor friend in attendance. Her birth was natural and without complication, just like the other births that occurred on the Breaks Ranch every year. As Laura came into the world the wee hours of Monday morning, we, were the happiest two people on planet Earth.

Eight hours later that Monday morning, Ann, still groggy from the night's excitement, answered the phone from bed, expecting the call to be from another relative, as the news of our joy circulated the family grapevine.

It was Deloris, the buyer from Western Farmers. Ann bubbled over with the good news of the birth of our baby daughter. Deloris, who had practically become family during the previous exciting few weeks, shared our joy with a few tears and sniffles of her own over the phone. Then she said, "Honey, are you sitting down?"

"What?" Ann asked.

"I'm serious," Deloris answered.

"Yeah, I'm sitting," Ann replied.

"Western Farmers just filed Chapter 11 bankruptcy this morning. All bill payments are on hold. We can't issue a single check. It is total panic here at headquarters," Deloris sobbed.

"What?" Ann asked in shock.

"We're broke. Western Farmers can't pay its bills. All I know is the court is appointing a trustee, and all our assets are frozen."

"But wait a minute," Ann stammered. "We just delivered that whole truckload of games to you just two days ago on Saturday. Plus all those other games, your total bill for all the games we've sold you is up to over $24,000. It was supposed to get paid this week," Ann's voice cracked.

"I know, sweetie," Deloris sobbed, "it's complete chaos here. None of us at my level had any idea that this bankruptcy was coming. It was a complete surprise to everybody in operations. We all knew we were having a few problems, but this ... Well, I've got to get off ... I thought you should hear it from me ... Sorry, kid," and she hung up.

Ann set the phone down next to the daybed in the living room where Laura, only a few hours old, lay quietly sleeping. As the news of this monumental blow sank in deep to the bone, Ann picked up our newborn and tenderly held her close. Soon tears of desperation fell on our baby's blanket.

My joy as I looked at them, the joy of the birth of our long-awaited daughter, was able to prop me up on the outside, but on the inside I felt more frightened and lost than I'd ever been in my whole life. Just as we had been lifted to the crest of success, we were suddenly dashed to the ground. It was cruel and unexpected, and I felt as if fate had turned against us.

10

The Winter of '80

• • • • • • • • • • • • • • • • • •

Despite our shellshock, we plunged ahead in sort of a blind daze, trying to keep at arm's length the full impact of what Western Farmers' bankruptcy meant to us. We couldn't quit or turn back. We could only go forward. And wishing would not make it so, no matter how badly we needed the cash — the $24,000 — that had been torn from our grasp by the store's failure.

Doing business from the boondocks always provided many challenges, and we met them the best we could. One big problem was the road to our place, running fifteen miles out from town. It became rough going when the weather got bad. The wind-driven snow, pushed back daily by the county road-grader, however, rarely deterred the UPS man. From Thanksgiving weekend on, chained up, he drove daily out to the ranch to pick up the orders we had ready to ship. The mountain of pre-cut cardboard mailers and games in our living room continued to shrink as we broke down, for individual shipment, the case packs I hauled home from Goodwill.

When the response to our magazine ads got rolling, we drove to town daily to get the mail. We used Goldendale as our business address because anyone trying to find the phone number of the Weekend Farmer Company by asking (509) information under the name of Centerville, our tiny rural post office, would have drawn a blank from the operator or, worse, a referral to Washington's other area code under Centralia. After negotiating with the postmaster, we eventually got our Goldendale mail delivered to our Centerville address.

The extensive media coverage we received locally drove sales wild in both The Dalles and Goldendale. In The Dalles we sold 2,500 games to a town of 12,000 people. We even sold sixty-five games in Bickleton, a town with a population of about fifty. As the word spread, I got calls from radio newsmen asking for an interview over the phone from as far away as St. Johns, Newfoundland, Canada.

In December, a regional correspondent for the *Washington Post* called me. He saw our story in the *Yakima Herald* when it hit the AP wire. He said his editor wanted to do a piece on *The Farming Game*, and on December 28, the Washington Post printed the article. From that exposure, an editor at People magazine called. She was doing a review of the best new games of the year for the "Picks and Pans" section and wanted a look at *The Farming Game*. Of the 2,500 new games that had come out on the market, *The Farming Game* was headed for their top ten new games spot. *Changing Times* magazine followed with a spread on our game for their February issue.

We were flying high on news coverage. Paper after paper picked us up. The reason was simple: editors had newspapers to fill with news every day. The press is usually starved for good news, especially good news about agriculture, our nation's largest industry. Farming is always a tough subject to report on when times are bad, and in the late seventies times were worse than bad; they were rotten. In fact times were the worst for America's farmers since the Great Depression, with third- or fourth-generation farms going bankrupt. Reporters from all types of media saw *The Farming Game* as I hoped they would, as a means of telling our story in a fresh and different format. I watched with great interest two years earlier when the national press corps made the inventor of the Pet Rock rich with the free exposure they gave to his silly little gift. There was a small chance they might do the same for us.

Then the fan letters started coming in. Some were saying: "*The Farming Game* has *Monopoly* beat by a mile!" Others reported they thought our game was a classic; and what was a proud papa to do but believe them? As the public lavished praise on my game, our sense of accomplishment grew, while at the same time, Ann sagged under the increasing pressures of running *The Farming Game* as a business.

The Western Farmers bankruptcy destroyed any hope of making a profit on our first edition. And it was completely uncertain, as highly leveraged as we were, that even if we sold every game, if we could borrow enough money to print a second edition to try to recoup our bankruptcy losses.

In the first six weeks of production we sold 7,000 copies of *The Farming Game*. Our big Christmas-sales success in The Dalles, where we sold enough games during the holiday season to put one in every fourth house, kept my imagination reeling. I was pie-eyed with dreams of replicating that kind of success in a big city like Chicago or New York.

We got letters and articles and orders from all over the country. I got phone calls from *The Farming Game* fanatics who were letting their Christmas dinner get cold as they argued over the slightly ambiguous first-edition *Farming Game* rules. For the final say-so, they decided to call the inventor himself to rule on a debatable point. I did my best to settle their disputes while my own Christmas dinner cooled.

It was clear that we had to continue to push *The Farming Game* after the Christmas season ended. So we signed up for the Portland Gift Show being held at Portland's convention center on January 4, 5 and 6 to exhibit our game. Fresh from the Christmas-sales success, I was primed to introduce our product to the mass market-place and sell our game into stardom. The New York Toy Fair is the granddaddy of fairs for the toy industry, but prac-tically every big city has its own event for regional retailers who couldn't attend the show in the Big Apple. At the last minute, Ann's brother Willy, who was between careers as a pro ski racer, fight promoter, building contractor, and tavern owner, signed on with us to be the sales manager of our fledgling company. He agreed to help me with the upcoming Portland show.

The Farming Game's booth stuck out like a sore thumb, a hick among the slicksters. The smooth profes-sional displays manned by the big manufacturers and distributors were quite a contrast to our booth decorated with hay bales, an old horse harness, stacks of the game, and a big sign that said:

IN BUSINESS ONLY SIX WEEKS
7,000 SOLD!

My plan, during the show, was to change the sales numbers on the sign as they multiplied, just like hamburger places did. I figured that with our media exposure, surely the retailing world was just waiting to beat a path to our door to buy my better mousetrap!

The first day at the Portland Gift Show was a real disappointment. We watched the buyers march by without even slowing, their official ID badges flashing. We hardly wrote an order. Willy and I pitched *The Farming Game* as best we could. The infectious enthusiasm of our success with small-town buyers was tough to transfer in a two-minute sales pitch. We made some sales to individual store owners, but it was obvious after the first few hours of the Gift Show that we probably weren't going to write many of those big orders to chain stores as we hoped. The only buyers who were stopping at our booth and taking the time to peruse our wares were the operators of little mom-and-pop stores that came to the Gift Show from the boondocks like ourselves on a buying holiday. As far as we could tell, the big buyers never even made it down to our end of the convention center.

Our second day at the Gift Show was better, but not by much. I knew before we went that the Gift Show was going to be part of a learning curve required for success in our new business. When activity at our booth was slow, I left Willy in charge and took off on a scouting mission to walk the huge show and check out the knee-deep merchandise. More important, I picked the brains of the sales reps in neighboring booths on subjects on which I was awfully green, such as how to close a deal.

After the second day of the show, which closed at six p.m., Willy and I drove home through the winter darkness to the Breaks Ranch. The winter weather in the Columbia Gorge that evening wasn't bad, so the drive was uneventful until we got home.

Kurt had come over from The Dalles to feed our cows and visit his new niece the first two days I was away at the Gift Show. The temperature had been above freezing both days, causing the soggy ground to thaw. During the second day's feeding, Kurt got our pickup stuck up to the axles in a sea of mud 300 yards from the road. Before he went back to The Dalles, he jacked the truck up and put old boards under the tires, ready to drive on should the ground refreeze during the night. I hoped if the temperature cooperated, in the morning I could drive the truck out of the slop to civilization.

One of my older stifle-hipped cows, one we planned to sell to cover our *Farming Game* bills, went down in the confusion around the mired pickup. Eighty-five cows and almost as many yearlings were fighting over the hay-loaded pickup. The crippled cow had been trampled. When I got to the field, she was lying dead in the mud near the truck, her eyes already pecked out by the hungry crows.

My mother-in-law Betty was at the ranch for a visit. She felt uneasy about my leaving her daughter alone while I went to the Gift Show. She was worried about Ann coping with a three-week-old baby and two toddlers, in the middle of nowhere, three miles from the nearest neighbor, midwinter with livestock to tend. Kurt wasn't able to feed the livestock on day three of the gift show. Wayne, a friend who lived down at Klickitat, promised to cover feeding that day, so Ann and her mom wouldn't have to concern themselves with bucking bales and feeding the herd. I tossed and turned all night thinking of the big problems Wayne would have feeding cows if I couldn't get the pickup out of the mud.

I woke up to frost at five the next morning. Without breakfast, I dressed, went straight to the field, and walked

out to my mired pickup truck. The ground had frozen
slightly during the night; it had firmed up the mud enough
to support my weight as I walked across it. I started my
truck and let it warm up for the challenge ahead. I gritted
my teeth, put the engine in gear, and poured the coal to it.
The truck skipped, bounced, and spun as all four wheels
churned across the half-frozen slime. I kept the pedal to the
metal until I had the truck safely on the county road. At six-
thirty, Willy and I left for Portland for the final day of the
Gift Show, which was slated to open two hours later.

Business the last day of the Gift Show was poor, but it
got a lot worse at noon when it started to sleet and then
snow in Portland. The bad weather prompted buyers to
leave the Gift Show in droves, and it became obvious that
day three was going to be our worst sales effort yet. By one
p.m., the convention center was a ghost town, and an hour
later Willy and I were packed and headed for home.

I was worried as I left Portland because, from the
amount of snow on the ground, I knew the Columbia Gorge
east of me was going to be a bear. My front-wheel-drive
station wagon had studded snow tires, and the bales of hay
we used for our booth, along with the rest of the show
props, were in the back of the car for ballast. The
snowstorm grew more and more intense as I neared
Troutdale, a small town fifteen miles east of Portland at the
mouth of the Gorge. It was snowing so hard that the
afternoon light was blotted out and traffic slowed to ten
miles an hour, the cars in front of me visible only as blurs
in the grey whiteness. Ahead, the flashing lights of a
highway patrol vehicle cut dim strokes through the blizzard.
As I slowed to a stop, I noticed that the flakes were so thick
I couldn't even make out the face of the patrolman as he
directed all traffic off the highway at the Troutdale exit.

Highway I-84 was closed through the Gorge. I couldn't get home to the Breaks Ranch tonight. The only option that made sense to me was to grab a motel room at Troutdale, which I did.

The desk clerk said that it must be my lucky day as he handed me the key to his last room. The highway had been closed only fifteen minutes.

As the motel man turned on the No Vacancy sign, I thought to myself, I may be inconvenienced overnight, but the cows were already fed for the day, and I should be able to get home in time to feed them tomorrow. I turned on my motel room TV and flopped down on the bed to catch a weather report. The storm on the satellite photos showed a bank of dense clouds that was about 2,500 miles wide. The travelers' advisory reported that the storm was officially upgraded to blizzard. I called home to Ann, and Betty answered the phone. She let me know in no uncertain terms that I was to get myself home to my responsibilities at the ranch and newborn baby daughter pronto, snow or no snow. Ann couldn't come to the phone because she was down at the barn, after trudging through the foot-and-a-half of new snow to feed the horses, bulls, and the replacement heifers. Betty said she would have Ann call me back when she got in.

When Ann returned my call a few hours later, I discovered that Willy, my partner at the Gift Show, had made it home to Seattle just in the nick of time, before I-5 was closed and downtown Seattle was totally paralyzed. Ann, at her maternal best, was full of soothing sympathy for my roadhouse imprisonment. Her report was mostly about our wonderful new daughter, Laura, who spent the day being the world's most perfect baby. The chores on the ranch were taken care of for the meantime, but there was no telling what tomorrow might bring.

The snow continued without letup for two more days. Reports said Cascade Locks, at the wettest part of the Columbia Gorge, twenty-five miles east of my motel-cell, received up to nine feet of snow. At home, the storm dumped about five feet of the white stuff. The Breaks Ranch was snowbound. The road grader had been out to the Breaks only once, the first day of the blizzard. That night there was a windstorm that blew the snow into ten-foot drifts and made all road travel impossible. Snow removal was now bulldozer work. The entire Northwest was paralyzed by the storm.

My wife and mother-in-law needed help. I didn't dare call Earl and Helen because I knew they had their own livestock crisis to deal with. I called a neighbor who lived about five miles from the ranch who had promised me he'd lend a hand if Ann and her mother needed any help while I was away. He was a guy I had nicknamed Grain Boy, a vegetarian in cow country. He had bought his land with an organic farm in mind and found out after a few tough seasons in Horseshoe Bend that raising cattle was the highest and best use of his land. So, vegetarian or not, he eventually went out and bought some cows. I always seemed to be the one he called if he had a cow with a bad eye or some other malady which required that the critter be manhandled. Grain Boy had no cattle-handling facilities of his own, no squeeze chute or a crowding alley, just a rickety corral built onto the front of the old milking shed with only one fencepost solid enough to snub a cow up to.

Grain Boy, like everyone else in a three-state area, was snowbound. He told me over the phone that the snow was so deep that he and his wife had not even been able to make it as far as his mailbox up on the road. He said there was no way he could be of much assistance at our place until the storm let up. He promised that as soon as he dug himself out at home he would help Ann and Betty with our livestock feeding problem.

We were wintering through most of our yearling calves to be sold in the spring. Our herd, including the new babies, just starting to come, and the yearlings, made over one hundred seventy mouths to feed. In Ann's weakened condition, just three weeks after childbearing, there was no possible way she could buck the hay needed to feed those cows. It was physically all Ann could do just to break trail through the chest-deep snow and get our barnyard animals fed. That short tour of barnyard duty took an hour and a half, and when Ann returned to the house, she was completely exhausted.

The haystack which fed the cow herd was located right next to their timber-sheltered winter feeding grounds about a mile up the hill from our house. The stack was separated from the feeding area by a barbed-wire fence that kept the cows from mauling the stack and wasting five times as much feed as they ate. Our normal method of feeding was to load the hay on the pickup truck, drive it out into the field, and toss it off on the ground, a section at a time. Our four-wheel-drive truck, though chained up on all four wheels, had become hopelessly mired in the deep snow the first day of the storm. So the job of getting my cows fed by hand fell to my mother-in-law, the only able-bodied adult left on the ranch.

Betty is an extraordinary woman, though at times justifiably critical of me. Even though she was born, bred and schooled to life in the world of the upper crust, Betty was by no means a hothouse flower. She was equally at home dining with the Rothschilds at a villa in France as she was paddling a canoe in the wilds of northern Canada. Betty was a phenomenal natural athlete. She had been golf and tennis champion at Seattle clubs for several years. She was an expert skier, a crack shot with a shotgun, camper, and world traveler. In addition to her athletic prowess, she possessed a sharp intellect and broad fields of interests.

Luckily, Betty brought her cross-country skis with her when she came to visit, planning to stop off and do a little skiing near Wenatchee on her way back to Seattle when I returned from the Gift Show. She put on her skis and broke trail through the snowdrifts skiing up the steep road the mile to our cows. She carried wire cutters and Ann's work gloves in her parka pockets. When she got to the stack, the first job ahead of her was digging out the hay bales by hand from under the heavy blanket of snow. Once the hay was uncovered, she cut the bale wires and carried the hay in individual armfuls to the fence through chest-deep powder. Over the fence it went, to the frenzied cows on the other side jostling one another to get to the prize. Betty kept at it, tossing hay until her arms hung weary with the drudgery of throwing two tons of hay over the fence.

Our cows had been spring-calving when we bought them, but Ann and I decided that it made more sense with the range conditions on the Breaks Ranch to calve them in the fall. If our calves were born in the fall they would be big enough to better utilize our ranch pasture,which starts to come on in March. At four months of age, the calf's fourth stomach, the rumen, has developed to the point that it can utilize roughage efficiently, getting the full digestive use from the forage. Since our pastures were always dry grass by mid-June, we had range conditions a fall calf could make the best use of.

Cows have the same gestation period as humans: nine months. To move our cows' calving dates from spring to fall we had one of two choices: 1) we could sneak them two or three weeks toward fall each year for about five years; or 2) leave them unbred for six months once, and lose half a year's production. Since we couldn't afford the better plan number two, we chose plan number one to back up the calving dates to fall, risking calf births in the dead of winter for three or four consecutive seasons.

Unfortunately the massive snowstorm struck in the middle of our second year of moving calving backward through the winter toward fall. Our calving season had just started, and our half-dozen new babies mired in deep snow struggling to stick close to their mothers for protection. Two of the youngest were trampled to death in the eager assault on the hay Betty's first morning feeding. The manual labor of feeding the cows through the deep snow was so exhausting that when she finally skied back to the house, it was all she could do to peel off her clothes and collapse into the bath.

As a result of normal planning on our part, Ann, her mother, and the kids had plenty to eat during the snowstorm. We made a practice to be prepared in the wintertime with plenty of meat in the freezer, a sack of hard red wheat for our grain mill, and a pantry full of home-canned fruit and vegetables. Since our water supply came from a gravity-fed cistern that flowed even if electricity was cut off at the pump, there was no danger of a shortage. There was ample firewood in our woodshed to keep the house warm. So, had there been no cows to feed, the blizzard of 1980 would have been a memorable family adventure for Ann and her mom, completely snowbound with the kids. Ann and Betty endured the storm as best they could, with my mother-in-law carrying the brunt of ranch chores on her shoulders.

My motel didn't have a restaurant, but there was one right next door at the Burns Brothers Truck Stop. Their parking lot was jammed full with about three hundred semi-trucks. All 300 truck engines in the lot idled, the engines kept running to prevent restarting problems in the freezing weather. Over hotcakes and coffee the truckers tallied the pooled resources marooned in the big rigs outside. Three semis carried frozen vegetables; two others were trans- porting hanging beef. There was a load of Wisconsin cheese the trucker swore was bound for an Oregon cheese factory, and there was a half-full Frito-Lay truck. We had plenty of provisions in the parking lot to keep us all going for at least six months.

At long last the snow finally stopped during the morning of the fourth day. The leaden ceiling in Troutdale started to rise and show patches of daylight through cracks in the threatening fluff. At ten a.m., there was word that the snowplows were working their way out I-84 toward our stranded outpost. Starting the first day I was snowed in, I borrowed the official motel-office snow shovel three times a day and dug and redug a path around my car. I wanted to be snow free and ready to go the minute the blizzard let up and the snowplows opened the street that went by the parking lot.

The snow had been heavy all over the Northwest, and all the major highways had reopened except the one I needed: I-84 through the Columbia Gorge. Reports said that, because of massive snows, Interstate-84 was closed indefinitely and might not reopen for a week. In order to get home, I had to drive back to Portland, then make my way north on I-5 to Seattle. From there I would head east over three mountain passes to make a 400-mile detour to the Goldendale Valley.

My trip over the next eleven hours was a white-knuckle nightmare. The weather turned bitterly cold as I crossed into Eastern Washington. I stopped only once six hours after starting, for a tank of gas and a stretch. Ten minutes later, I pulled out of the gas station with two candy bars and a vendo-sandwich for my dinner. Already on my trip I had witnessed three accidents, observed a dozen narrow misses, and covered hundreds of miles of highway littered with stalled vehicles. Umptahnam Pass south of Ellensburg was covered with packed ice from the crosswinds driving snow across the roadway. The ice made the roadway almost as rough as driving cross-ties on a railroad.

Going through the Yakima Valley I had a narrow miss, as a '68 Chevy Impala went careening out of control right in front of me. I swerved just enough to avoid him by inches as he went off through the snowbank into the bushes that grew in the median between the oncoming lanes.

At midnight I finally peaked Satus Pass, where Highway 97 crosses the Simcoe Mountains, and headed downhill into the Goldendale Valley. When I pulled into the parking lot of the grocery store in Goldendale, it was just the second time I stirred from the driver's seat since that morning. After eleven hours of intense maneuvering behind the wheel, I had to straighten a finger to operate the dial on the payphone to call home.

Ann's relief was evident when she answered the phone. While she was glad that I was only fifteen miles from home, she warned me that I couldn't get through to the ranch. "They haven't gotten out here with the roadgrader yet," she said. "Horseshoe Bend Road is still blown shut. Even Grain Boy hasn't made it over here to help Mom feed the cows and he lives almost next door. I don't see any way possible you can make it home tonight."

But I was determined to make my goal. A half an hour later and only five miles out from town, my car plowed through its last snowdrift and mired. I could drive no further. The night sky was broken clouds over a full moon; it was windless at ground level, with the mercury at about twenty degrees. With the car stalled, my remaining option was to walk, though dressed in my city clothes and a pair of tennis shoes on my feet. Before I left the safety of the car to start my midnight trek through the snowdrifts, I found a roll of shipping tape and taped my pant legs to my shoes. The leggings did a reasonably good job of keeping the snow out of my socks as I trudged off through the drifts heading west toward home.

After 200 yards of hiking, I was warm as toast and ready to unzip my coat. In the ten more miles I had to go to reach the Breaks Ranch there were only four houses I would pass. I walked homeward in total darkness. Though windless at ground level, the clouds above were moving swiftly, headed east a few thousand feet up. At times they totally blocked out the moonlight. I staggered on westward, sinking in the snow and cursing the dead flashlight I left in the glovebox. Our road, which had been plowed only the first day of the storm, was now packed with drifts eight to ten feet high in places. I stumbled through them in the dark, as step by step I trudged closer to home.

After two hours, I was growing exhausted as I neared Grain Boy's place and made the decision that I had walked far enough for that night. I had made it! I could easily walk the rest of the way home in the morning, feeding my cows as I went. So I trudged down the long, drifted driveway into Grain's place with a feeling of satisfaction, knowing I was now close enough to home that I could finally relieve Betty, from her cattle-feeding chores. As I walked down the driveway, I realized I couldn't wait to see the expression on Grain Boy's face when he opened the door of his little ramshackle cabin.

It was nearly three a.m. when I banged on Grain Boy's front door with all my might. I woke the whole household out of a dead sleep. His jaw dropped and he flushed when he opened the door, as if he'd seen a ghost. We had talked just that morning when I was still miles away, snowbound in Troutdale. After a few moments of confusion he finally invited me in, and my day's travels were at an end. After calling home to give Ann my final report, I borrowed Grain Boy's sleeping bag and in a few minutes was dead asleep on the living room floor.

11

When You're Bucked Off, You Gotta Get Back On

• • • • • • • • • • • • • • • • • •

To our delight, game sales continued briskly beyond Christmas. Most people who had gotten *The Farming Game* as a present tried it out and liked it so much that their enthusiasm sold another game to a brother, cousin, or next-door neighbor. *The Farming Game* began getting a lot of use in high schools, as vocational-agriculture teachers immediately recognized it as a fun way to teach farm economics. By March, we sold out the last games of our first edition and were grappling with what to do next.

The Western Farmers Co-op bankruptcy and their unpaid debt to us created a nasty $24,000 hole in our borrowing power, a hole the size of the total purchase price of our first farm. Under Chapter 11 bankruptcy law, the unsecured debts of Western Farmers could accrue no interest or late charges as it languished unpaid. The co-op was being reorganized under the court-appointed trustee, and its assets were being sold off to service its overextended debt. Just how much we would eventually recover, if anything, was still anyone's guess. As an unsecured creditor, we were at the liquidator's mercy. Since it was still operating, the co-op would continue to sell our games they'd never paid for, and we could do nothing about it.

Run size rules the economics of the printing business. The more impressions you print at one time, the cheaper the job is per each. Ann's calculations showed that printing the next edition of games should be at least 25,000 to reduce the costs low enough to provide for a profit margin broad enough for us to pursue advertising and promotion. It was not easy selling our oversized, high-quality games in the retail world of mass-produced, low-cost boardgames. The competition from other board games priced at $10 made it tough for us to compete with a product that sold for almost twice as much.

Our game was out of step. Buyers for the chain stores just didn't seem to have much time to waste on a one-product-manufacturing small fry like me. Not when they could be talking to a rep who handles two dozen lines.

The Farming Game might be the greatest thing since Velcro in our eyes, but we needed to get it on the stores' shelves, giving people the opportunity to buy it and try it and judge for themselves. We were still getting fan mail daily from *The Farming Game* fanatics from all over the country. The letters were from all kinds of people — from nine-year-olds to university professors and anyone in between. The success we'd had so far had been kicked off by our exposure in the media, but it was word of mouth that was keeping it going.

Our huge winter snow stayed on until March, when the weather turned rainy. The spring of 1980 brought the best pasture season on our south-facing canyon hillsides that we'd had since we moved to the Breaks Ranch. The green hills were alive with the sounds of water gurgling from wet springs which had been silent during our annual dry spell. The iridescent Mountain Bluebirds came back to nest after their winter's absence, a sure sign winter was finished and that we all made it safely through to spring.

The winter had been hard on our cattle. When we turned them out to pasture the end of the third week in March, they never looked worse. But I knew after a few weeks on our rich spring pasture, they soon would be fat and glossy again.

With the first week in April came a surprise. Our mail brought us a letter from the Fox brothers of Illinois. This was far more than just a fan letter. Brother Steve, a veterinarian just discharged from the Navy in Bremerton, Washington, had seen *The Farming Game* on the shelf of a Western Farmers Co-op outlet. He decided that the game would make a perfect Christmas gift for his brother Dick, who ran the family farms in Illinois and was also district manager of a large Midwest farm supply co-op. Steve was right — Dick went wild for our game and played it with just about everybody in a two-county area. In so doing, he became convinced that *The Farming Game* was destined for the big time. Dick convinced a third brother, Mike, a CPA and a corporate treasurer for a firm based in Chicago, that if the Fox family, could acquire the marketing rights to *The Farming Game*, they would be managing the sales of the game that was surely the successor to Monopoly.

The Fox brothers' letter stated that they wanted to fly out and meet with us at our earliest convenience to discuss their involvement in the marketing of our invention. They said they saw a huge market for *The Farming Game* in the Midwest alone. Besides selling the game in stores, they believed it was a perfect fund raiser for clubs like the 4-H and FFA. They thought that everyone in the United States could use a *Farming Game,* or maybe two; one for the vacation cabin and one in the game closet at home for when friends came over. The Fox brothers said they believed annual sales for our game should easily reach into the hundreds of thousands. They were convinced my invention was so good that once the public tried *The Farming Game*, it would be a runaway success, and the Foxes wanted part of the action.

The three brothers flew into Portland to meet with us the following week. We got along well. Their straightforward style, combined with their credentials, convinced us that they could and would do everything they promised. Within a month we signed a contract. The Fox brothers would take the territory east of the Rockies as their exclusive marketing domain. Dick would quit his job as district manager to work full time selling the game. The Foxes put up the money and ordered a forty-foot container load of *The Farming Game* shipped by rail to Chicago ASAP.

Ann and I were on cloud nine. Our game had been on the market only six months, and already it was headed for the big time. If the optimistic sales projections were met, we would open a second production line at a Goodwill somewhere in the Midwest to save on transportation costs. The people at Goodwill were ecstatic with our success and remodeled their contract assembly area to better produce our product. They were ready and willing to swing into full production, putting about twenty people to work full time on our project.

We were cookin'! *The Farming Game* was hot! The prospects never looked more promising; our future had finally arrived. In reality, we were in greater need of more financing than ever before in our lives. The unpaid debt owed us by Western Farmers hung like a millstone around our necks. The Weekend Farmer Company needed a capital infusion in the worst way to make our bank's borrowing formula work to produce our second run of games. Help came to us in the person of none other than Ann's mother, Betty. Without our prompting she offered to become a limited partner in *The Farming Game* and replace the cash flow from the Western Farmers' bankruptcy.

When the Fox brothers ordered a second container of farm games, it seemed that we were definitely on a greased track to success. Little did we know that halfway around the world the Russians were invading Afghanistan and that President Jimmy Carter's response was going to be a grain embargo that would hurt American farmers far worse than it hurt the Russians.

With Betty's cash infusion and the Foxes' orders, we were able to secure financing for a production run of 25,000 copies of *The Farming Game*. The trick, of course, was to sell these games as quickly as possible before the interest on the loan to build the inventory ate up all the savings that came from a larger production run. It seemed like a good time to pay a personal call on our suppliers back East.

We weren't going to do any more business with Horse Puckey and company. I wanted to visit the biggest game board manufacturer in the country, on the off chance that the Foxes were really onto something and *The Farming Game* sales would go through the roof as the brothers projected. Colorforms, the company that manufactured the vinyl acreage stamps, also had their headquarters in the East. The trip also was a good excuse to visit Princeton and, while I was there, to see a few old friends.

Hay season was approaching, and I knew that if I didn't go east before the first of May, I wouldn't be able to get away until midsummer, too late to deal with the manufacturers about our growing production needs. I booked a flight to Newark.

New Jersey seemed quite strange to me after my ten-year absence. It was so flat I felt closed in. I had grown used to promontories where I could stare down into deep canyons and out across great vistas. New Jersey's bustling development wedged into the thick deciduous forest was a far cry from the place I now called home. And I was surprised to see New Jersey was greener with more farmland and less of an industrial cesspool, than I remembered.

The ivy-covered walls of Princeton town and the gentle, arched, stone bridge over Lake Carnegie carried an air of permanence and history that I found I missed living in the West. The University's buildings of stone and mortar emitted an aura that, by comparison, made my existence out on the Breaks of the Klickitat River Canyon seem quite transitory. We were only the seventh family that had owned the Breaks Ranch since it had been homesteaded in the 1870s, and three of those families had gone broke. It was wonderful to visit my old hometown, but after a day or two I was itching to get back to the wild spaces of the West.

I had an appointment with my contact at Colorforms for first thing Monday morning. During our many phone conversations involving the game, he had proved himself to be a nice guy who took a personal interest in our headlong pursuit of *The Farming Game*. I was not surprised at the beginning of our meeting when he asked, with obvious concern showing on his face, how my family was.

"They are just fine. Little Laura's growing fast; she's crawling and happy as a clam. Ann is holding up amazingly well under the workload. As for the boys...."

He interrupted, "Then they escaped the volcano blast in good shape?"

"The what?" I asked, completely stunned.

"Mount St. Helens blew up yesterday! Didn't you know?" he asked unbelievingly.

"Oh my God! May I use your phone? I was at a barbecue all day yesterday, and I haven't seen or heard the news all weekend." He handed me the phone across the desk. "St. Helens has been huffing and puffing for months. Our ranch is only about forty miles away, due east of it, right in the path of the prevailing winds," I answered in anguish, while dialing his phone.

A ball of tension started to form in my guts as a recorded message told me, time and again, all circuits were busy and to try my call again later, thank you.

"Tell me what happened," I pleaded, hanging up the busy phone in shock.

"From what I heard, there was a massive eruption that blew the top right off the mountain. There are huge floods and mudslides on some rivers, and it's raining ash hundreds of miles downwind, over Montana now, I think. It's been on every newscast for the last twenty-four hours. I'm surprised that you could have missed it," he said sympathetically.

I furiously redialed my home number, but the damn circuits were still busy. I gave up phoning and tried to muddle through my business appointment, the obligatory plant tour, and a lunch that I could not even taste because my mind was with Ann at the ranch. Thoughts of my family choking to death as the volcanic dust rained out of the sky was too much for me to bear. A few weeks earlier, Mount St. Helens had burped a little plume of volcanic ash that rained down across our place, a tiny taste of a full-blown eruption. The ash fell in a layer like heavy dew. We spent the entire day huddled in the bedroom with sheets hanging in the doorways of our partially completed house. Our house was not yet tight enough to keep the suffocating dust out. It seemed to seep in through every crack and crevice. The wind was blowing hard that day, and the fine volcanic dust blew wherever it chose. Like Dustbowlers of years past, we waited with the kids in our bedroom with handkerchiefs over our mouths and noses for hours until the dust storm subsided and the gritty residue settled to the ground. The next day it seemed the volcanic ash was like a frost that wouldn't melt. A week later, a rain shower washed part of it away, but the ash reappeared uninjured in dirty rivulets as the moisture dried up.

My one small taste of Mount St. Helens' ash made me fear how miserable life must be for all of Central Washington now choking in it. I listened to the news reports on the car radio driving down the New Jersey Turnpike. The city of Yakima, seventy miles east and north of Mount St. Helens, was blanketed by three inches of coarse ash. Ritzville, in the center of Washington State, received six inches of fine volcanic ash. The ash was still falling hundreds of miles downwind as the cloud moved east with the jetstream. More than a cubic mile of mountaintop had been vaporized and spewed into the air. Listening to the continually updated news reports of the devastating volcanic eruption from a car in a traffic jam 3,000 miles away accentuated my feelings of helplessness.

As I drove through the flatlands of New Jersey, I cringed at Dante-like visions of scenes that might be taking place with my home and family at the ranch that very minute. Fresh reports continued over the car radio about the unbelievable devastation wrought by Mount St. Helens. Transportation was completely paralyzed in Central

Washington. The threat of further eruptions hung like the sword of death over the entire region.

The governor called out the National Guard and asked for a federal disaster declaration to start the full-scale relief operation going. On the west side of the volcano, where there had been no ash fallout, there were instead flash floods and racing mudslides. Luckily, most of the devastation was confined to a sparsely populated part of the Cascades.

I tried again with no luck to get a call through to Ann when I finally reached my mother's house, after fighting my way through typical rush-hour traffic. I felt as helpless as a bug skewered with a pin. Chasing *The Farming Game* all over the country was putting my family and ranching operation at risk in new ways I couldn't predict and seemed powerless to resist. My torment continued into the night, until finally near midnight I got my call through to home.

I learned that Ann and the kids were fine; the volcanic ash path was north of the Breaks Ranch by about fifteen miles! No matter our proximity to the mountain, the volcanic ash and its effects had missed us entirely! My cousin, who lived 550 miles downwind in Helena, Montana, had already called to see if we were all right. She reported they had gotten a heavy dusting of ash in Helena and couldn't believe that, living so close to the exploding mountain, we escaped completely. Mount St. Helens was rumbling ominously again, and scientists could offer no solid predictions about the mountain's future. The major eruption caught everyone by surprise, so for all anyone knew, another massive blow could happen tomorrow. Having been caught off guard just a few months before by the blizzard, and even though I knew my family was safe, Mount St. Helens gave me nightmarish dreams. I couldn't take the strain, so I cut short my stay in the East and flew back to my responsibilities.

The huge volcanic ash fall had been hell for many farmers. The affected were working around the clock trying to salvage their crops. The damage was everywhere and different to each crop affected. Some field crops were just plowed down, ash and all. Much of the 70,000 acres of fruit in the valley was in jeopardy of no crop at all if the ash wasn't removed quickly. Orchard owners were using the prop wash from helicopters to blow ash off the leaves of their trees. They found that too many hours without sunlight would cause the trees to drop the new fruit as a survival measure.

Cattle ranchers in the ash path had their spring range obliterated overnight, buried beneath the heavy grey mat. The cattle would have to be moved or fed hay while the grass tried to grow through the grit. It looked as though the dryland wheat growers were going to lose a whole year's crop in areas where the ash was so deep that it smothered the plants. Perhaps the worst hit were the irrigated alfalfa hay growers in the Columbia Basin. When the mountain blew, first-cutting alfalfa was just under way in the warmer parts of the Basin, but none of it had yet been baled. Approximately 40,000 acres of first-cutting hay was covered with ash. Not only was the crop ruined, but the farmers had a giant disposal problem of hauling the grimy hay out of the fields so they had a chance to make a saleable second cutting.

No dairyman or horse feeder would touch the ashed-on hay with a ten-foot pole. The price of quality hay, which had been $65 per ton a week before the mountain blew, jumped to $125 per ton for ash-free hay. What had started as a mediocre year for hay prices was now the highest hay price in Northwest history.

The heavy winter snows had saturated the soils on our ranch to their limit, and the young stands of alfalfa were poised to produce an excellent crop of high-quality hay. The alfalfa was in full bud, on the edge of coming to bloom when I started swathing. My phone was ringing off the hook with customers wanting a chance to buy my clean new crop of hay.

For the first time in years on the farm, I felt like I was in the driver's seat instead of being driven over. I was going to make a killing selling my hay! It was a new experience to have people begging to buy my alfalfa crop that wasn't even cut yet. I presold 150 tons of my hay to a swanky horse-training center near Seattle that I had been trying unsuccessfully to do business with before the eruption. Without hesitation they agreed to the price I was asking and were happy to get it. No self-respecting horse person wants dusty, moldy, or musty hay to feed their high-priced hayburners.

I put our baler in the field as soon as possible behind the swather. I had three good mornings of hay baling and had over 2,000 bales on the ground, about a day's work to put into a field stack with my bale wagon. The weather was warm and sunny when our hay trucker called to say he'd had mechanical trouble and would not be able to pick up the horse lady's first load until the following day. I decided to swath more of my fast-maturing hay and put off until the following day stacking the hay already baled. I knew I could easily stack the 650 bales to fill his thirty-ton truckload in just a few hours. That was Wednesday. Thursday morning before dawn, heavy clouds rolled in and it began to rain.

In June we normally average only 1.2 inches of rain for the entire month; and usually, a wind blows right behind any rainstorm and evaporates the moisture before it can do much damage to the hay. With our light, dryland hay windrows, we rarely ever had to turn over our rained-on hay to dry it enough to bale. The winds that follow spring and summer rains in the Gorge usually did that job quite efficiently. As I looked out the pickup window at my soggy hay Thursday morning, I felt a big twinge of guilt that I had not worked a little harder or a little smarter and stacked all that beautiful, high-priced hay that was already baled. The rain stood a chance of ruining by far the best hay crop I had ever produced out on the Breaks.

Sun and rain bleaching are the two prime enemies of quality hay in the windrow. The rule of thumb in our desert country is that, once the hay is safely in the bale, it will keep its quality lying out in the field for weeks under moderate meteorological abuse. When rain clouds loom, the cry is, "Get it in the bale," because properly dried baled hay can easily withstand an inch or so of rain with few real problems. That year the conventional wisdom was dead wrong. As Mount St. Helens' ash cloud was passing in the stratosphere high overhead, beginning its second orbital pass around the planet since the eruption, Thursday's rain dragged into Friday. The rain continued on Saturday and Sunday, until we received a full four-inch soaking. The rain clouds hung motionless over the Northwest for a week.

When the downpour finally ended the 2,000 bales sitting out in the field were totally ruined; and the hay, left in windrows lying on the ground, looked the color of a teabag that had been used for a week.

Hoping they might dry enough to be usable, over the next two weeks my boys and I rolled the rain-soaked bales over to a different side every few days. Each and every bale became a cube of rot. Not only wasn't it saleable, but so rotten I didn't dare feed it to my own cows the following winter. A choking fog of black mold spores flew into the air when a bale was broken open. The bales would have been worth more than $5 apiece if they had been picked up only one day earlier. But now they were nothing but compost. A sizable portion of my 1980 hay crop was now a garbage disposal problem.

The several hundred acres of our hay that lay still unbaled in the windrow eventually dried and was baled up. It was pretty sorry-looking stuff, but it was at least usable. I knew my cows would find the bleached, nasty-looking hay infinitely more appealing midwinter than a snowbank.

With a one-man dryland hay operation, the farmer must start cutting before the hay is quite ready, to guarantee that by the time he finishes, the last hay he cuts is not too overripe and steamy. The 200 acres of hay I had left uncut, which was bordering on overripe when the rains came, was now a tall, rank, tangled mess when the fields finally dried enough to start swathing again. I had plenty of company in the year's hay harvest disaster, but most of our neighbors also grew wheat or barley and were jumping for joy, since the heavy rains came at precisely the right time to fill out the grain heads with big, fat kernels. The full week of drizzle had practically guaranteed a bumper dryland grain harvest. It was the first season on the Breaks Ranch that we'd been without a wheat crop. I had planted over our last wheat field to grass and alfalfa hay that spring, so we were out of the wheat business just in time to miss the highest-yielding grain crop in a decade.

In the meantime, the Fox brothers were scurrying around all over the Midwest and making big noises in early summer. They used up their first trailerload of 7,000 copies of *The Farming Game* immediately and then ordered another. Western Farmers Co-op continued to order new games on a cash-only basis, though there was still no payment in sight on what they owed. We were doing a good mail-order business from our home and decided to place new ads in farm trade publications for the upcoming Christmas season.

The Farming Game was selling so well, in fact, that we calculated we would run out of games from our second printing way before Christmas. In July, we started planning for a second run of 25,000 to keep up with demand. The Fox brothers were doing everything they promised to make *The Farming Game* a big success. Dick had quit his job, and was cutting a wide swath across the farm belt. But due to a dry spell that gripped the Midwest, he was not having as easy a time selling *The Farming Game* as the brothers had anticipated.

By midsummer, with record dry weather throughout the Midwest, the Foxes' home base, the soybean crop was a disaster, and corn in a five-state region was severely hurting. I had not invented *The Farming Game* to become a toy salesman, and hooking up with the Fox brothers looked to me to be a dream come true. That was, at least, until the Midwest's 1980 corn crop followed the soybeans and dried up and blew away too.

12

The Omen

• • • • • • • • • • • • • • • • • •

Carter's grain embargo on Russia, imposed in 1980 to protest the Soviet Union's invasion of Afghanistan, cut the belly out of American grain prices. The whole agriculture community was stunned as the consequences of the multi-million-ton grain embargo rippled through a national farm economy depending on exports for 50 percent of its sales. In the Midwest, the severe drought in the same year cut crop yields so low that, combined with the rock-bottom prices, found solid farmers facing financial ruin.

The farm belt had been reasonably healthy and vigorous in 1979, though feeling the pinch of high inflation. But, the 1980 double whammy of embargo and drought brought on a wholesale collapse of farm values in all the Midwest rural communities that were the home base of the Fox brothers' sales campaign for *The Farming Game*.

Ann and I had been goaded into producing a second run of 25,000 games. The run was slated to cover the Fox brothers' projected orders, which dried up to nothing by early fall, as the Midwest battened down the hatches for hard times in the homeland. For farmers the times soon became as rough as any since the Great Depression. Twenty-five hundred farms were going out of business each week all across the country. The collateral effects of Carter's embargo destroyed prices for practically everyone engaged in farming; the drought in the Midwest just made it that much worse. The damnable dry weather was the straw that broke the farmer's back. The fallout resulted in many heart-rending auction sales of farms that had been in families for generations. Urban America saw the nightly news footage of the carnage in the countryside, while we who lived there watched firsthand as our friends and neighbors went broke one by one.

It was painfully obvious to Ann and me by Christmas 1980 that the Fox brothers weren't going to be able to move the huge inventory of games that we had built to cover the orders we'd been assured were forthcoming.

At the same time, to further compound our troubles, the nation was experiencing runaway, double-digit inflation. The Federal Reserve's answer was to double the interest rates and choke the problem to death. Suddenly the cost of our borrowed money soared from 12 percent to 22 percent, the highest interest rates in recorded business history. We were stocked to the gills with inventory and its associated debt at the worst possible moment. Our miscalculation of the number of games to produce set us on yet another collision course with bankruptcy. And, to speed up the crash, the interest meter was ticking at twice the normal rate gnawing away at our potential profits like uncontrolled rats in a grainery.

The message was clear: the only way out of this predicament was to sell our way out. It was imperative that

I hit the road immediately, and peddle *The Farming Game* however and wherever I could.

The Breaks Ranch and my family would have to learn to get along without me for a week or two at a time, as I signed up for agricultural winter trade shows all across the West. I didn't feel at all good about the thought of leaving the cows for weeks at a time in the dead of winter, but it was a risk we had to take. I found a more reliable person than Grain Boy to take care of the cows in my absence and hit the road in our station wagon crammed to the roof liner with games and booth materials.

I had not invented the game to become a salesman living on the road. But Ann, our firm voice of fiscal reality, told me in no uncertain terms that if I didn't become a salesman right quick and move a pile of our *Farming Game* inventory, we were goners. It was a race to the finish against the 22 percent interest on our combined loans ticking away like a timebomb. In a moment of weakness, I calculated the hourly wage I would have to earn to pay the interest on our mountain of debt. Much to my horror, I found I would have to make about $50 per hour, calculated on a forty-hour week, just to cover our growing tab at the bank. The financial pressure built to an intolerable level, and I feared that my blind ambition endangered our little family. I was distressed almost beyond measure. For weeks I tossed and turned, unable, even in exhaustion, to get a good night's sleep. I felt like a rat on a treadmill, my tongue hanging out, running to stay ahead of our crushing mountain of inventory.

My basic road plan was simple: I booked a three- or four-day agriculture show several hundred miles away, and then I stopped in every little town along the road on the way there. I would take a different route home and do the same thing on the way back. I found I could drive into most towns and be talking to the owner or manager of a store within minutes, and a few minutes later I could walk out the door with a check in hand for games I had sold. The ag shows were an opportunity for us to sell *The Farming Game* at retail prices to farm families directly. The shows were also a good source of potential distributors and contacts.

I rented booth space to exhibit in the winter ag shows in Portland; Spokane; Minot, North Dakota; Billings, Montana; and Colusa, California. My long hours on the road, sleeping in fleabag motels and living out of the car began to pay off. In my desperation, I turned into an aggressive salesman and got new accounts for *The Farming Game* daily. The games, sold well in store after store, and soon I acquired a grabbag of success stories to add to my sales pitch at the next store down the road. I toured much of the western U.S.A. with my station wagon and roof rack loaded to the limit with games. The income from the retail sales at the ag shows paid the expenses of my road trips. The repeat sales to new stores slowly ate away at the inventory that hung like a yoke around our necks.

A few weeks after the disastrous Portland Gift Show the previous winter, Ann's brother Willy, had temporarily tried his hand as the sales manager of the Weekend Farmer Company. He had taken a sales swing through the Rocky Mountain West. Willy sold *Farming Games* on days when it didn't conflict with his pro ski racing circuit. On that trip, Willy had shown the game at the MATE (Montana Agricultural Trade Exhibition) show in Billings, Montana. It was extremely successful. Montana loved our game, and Willy grossed several thousand dollars during the four-day show. He also landed a few small stores on that trip, and all of them had reordered at least once. Montana looked like paydirt. I booked the MATE show for the second year in hopes of mining that gold myself.

Willy had since retired as our sales manager, but he volunteered to go to the MATE show with me because he had fun there the year before, and besides, he was scheduled for a ski race in Montana about then anyway.

The MATE show was promising, in terms of foot traffic and enthusiastic buyers. The Civic Center was packed to overflowing with exhibitors. The nasty winter weather that met us, as we drove into Billings, did not deter the hardy Montana farmers and ranchers who came out every day in droves. Willy and I manned our booth ten hours a day, talking nonstop to the passersby, trying to sell each and every one a *Farming Game.* Selling our game to those folks was as easy as could be. It was also great fun for me, the inventor, to hear the rave reviews face to face from the satisfied customers, who bought to the game from Willy a year earlier.

Working the MATE show was very positive, a great release for my pent-up frustrations. Life on the road if you're young and single can be fun and exciting, but it felt increasingly empty without the daily contact with my wife and kids. Life on the road also required as much stamina as farming, because after ten hours of working the crowds, I followed my bachelor brother-in-law out partying with other sales reps we met at the show. Our favorites were the Quick brothers from Saskatoon, Saskatchewan. They manufactured a hydraulically driven grain bin auger called the Wheat Heart Bin Sweep. The brothers were single too and all full of go. They were great fun to b.s. with into the wee hours of the morning. The MATE show had many distributors and manufacturers from all over Canada and the U.S. The high-energy sales crowd from the show partied at a pace that I was in no shape to match. A wife, kids, a failing ranch, and my nose to the grindstone for years had left me very little time for training as a lounge lizard, but I tried really hard to keep up.

Until long after midnight, Willy and I swapped stories with the Canadians. The Quick boys were from the Republic of Western Canada, as it said on their baseball caps. They were having great fun baiting a sales rep from French-speaking Quebec, who had just finished telling a story with *National Enquirer*-like science-fiction overtones. I cleared my throat, callused by three show days of nonstop talking, and broke into a story of my own. The Omen.

The Farming Game received enthusiastic treatment from the local press during the MATE show, and a good-sized article appeared about *The Farming Game* in the Billings newspaper. I held interviews with two radio stations during my stay and had generally done anything I could think of that would create awareness of what I was up to. My story about *The Farming Game* was well known among the other sales folks at the show. Reps took in the other exhibits at the show during breaks, so they became familiar with each other's products and sales pitches.

My sales pitch came from real life. *The Farming Game* was an expression of that. The story of Annie's springtime ultimatum, and the invention six weeks later of *The Farming Game*, was well known by my small crowd of late-night revelers. I promised to tell them the full story, which I said began several months earlier in February, four months before the fateful hay-baling session that begat my game....

"February 9, 1979," I began, "all of the nation focused on the Goldendale Valley for one short moment. A total solar eclipse was scheduled for eight-fifteen a.m." On a hill north of town is the Goldendale Observatory, the largest telescope in the U.S.A. available for public use. The telescope was built by several men from Vancouver and situated near Goldendale to take advantage of the generally cloudless clarity of the Eastern Washington night skies. Also, our sparsely populated county did not generate much light pollution to affect the view of the heavens. National network news crews were camped out on Observatory Hill for coverage of the celestial event.

As it got closer and closer to the day of the eclipse, Ann and I kept getting phone calls and letters from friends inviting themselves to come view the eclipse from the our place. We weren't planning an event. In fact, if the eclipse wasn't happening right at home, it was highly doubtful, with the workload, the kids in diapers, and a ranch on the skids, that Ann and I would even cross the street to see one.

The sky was cloudy on eclipse eve when the guests arrived, just as I had predicted. The weather had been very warm for early February. It had rained nearly every day for three weeks and showed no signs of letting up. The creeks were running full. The small canyon that our home sits in was filled with the roar of the twenty-foot waterfall 200 yards from the house. The night before the big event, guests were packed everywhere in the house in their sleeping bags. There were about a dozen people upstairs in the unfinished loft, more in the living room and the basement, and a couple sleeping in the kitchen.

The solar eclipse was scheduled for precisely eight-fifteen a.m. Totality was to last two minutes and twenty seconds. All of our guests, those invited and those unannounced, descended on us for a show that wouldn't last as long as a good toothbrushing. The whole household was up early, buzzing with anticipation. Over coffee everyone discussed the upcoming event while I hurried around the barnyard doing chores, so I too could be free at the appointed time.

For viewing the eclipse, I chose a hill above the field where we feed our cows. The rise afforded an expansive view of the skies to the south, where the sun was scheduled to do its thing. The media hoopla surrounding the solar eclipse had doubled or tripled the population of the Goldendale area for the event. While ABC and NBC battled for supremacy on Observatory Hill, modern-day Druids maintained an all-night vigil at the replica of Stonehenge that sits on a lonely windswept bluff at Maryhill on the Columbia River.

Washington's Stonehenge was built in 1920 by Sam Hill, the visionary railroad man. Hill built the full-size replica as a memorial to Klickitat County's World War One dead. He was a Quaker and viewed the losses in Europe as yet another sacrifice of youth to the gods of war. It was believed at the time that the Stonehenge in England was once a site where the Druids practiced human sacrifice, though now it's considered to be a gigantic celestial timepiece.

Our viewing location at the Breaks Ranch was not nearly so dramatic as the scene at Stonehenge, with no people in flowing robes shaking bone rattles and chanting. At a quarter to eight, nearly thirty of us stood clustered on the hill in the middle of a large hayfield with not another person for miles in any direction. The clouds still hung low but had started moving slowly to the east, and at 8:05, like magic, the quadrant containing the sun opened to reveal clear blue sky!

I had fed our cows their hay on the ground next to our big stock pond about two hundred yards below our vantage point. I was curious if this event that so stirred the ancients would have any effect on bovines. As the minutes ticked away, the air grew very still and the light took on an ethereal glow. The brimming-full stock pond was as still as a five-acre sheet of glass which, from our vantage point, reflected the towering Ponderosa pines and beyond the cloud-laden northern sky. The sun's quadrant remained open as the cosmic event drew nearer.

A hush went over our group as people fingered their eye-protecting eclipse viewers. After hearing the PR campaign about protecting the retinas of the curious we made sure we had ample quantities of reflective mylar to stare at the eclipse through.

When the moon crossed into the sun's path minutes before totality, a fantastic, wave-like ripple of shadows rolled in quick succession across the hayfield. All thirty of us were reduced to monosyllables of amazement as the eclipse moved into totality. It was instantly as dark as night, a complete shock to our daylight-accustomed eyes. Everyone in the group focused on the view of the sun's corona through their protective visors, myself included. It lasted an incredible two short minutes as the moon inched its way across the face of the sun.

I was in rapture. The event was so dramatic, it was beyond comparison with any natural event I had ever witnessed. My face was pressed into my homemade viewer, transfixed by the experience, when suddenly, in the middle of the totality, a bird fell out of the sky and hit me in the side of the head, knocking off my Stetson! The bird, its fall softened by the brim of my hat, bounced off the ground and took off flying northeast. I was stunned, not by the blow, which had been miniscule, but by the improbability of the event! Perhaps an omen.

Soon, the earth returned to normal, and the sun regained its luster. The eclipse was over. Somewhere across the valley I knew the Druids were howling at the sky, and with the media and the crowds at Goldendale and at the Observatory, things were hopping like a three-ring circus. At the Breaks Ranch, we were all in a far more somber mood. The eclipse had been a soul-touching event that we all shared in our own individual ways. Our house guests soon vanished as suddenly as they appeared, and Ann and I were left alone again within a few hours of the event, still savoring the experience in memory.

"After that bird fell out of the sky," I told the barroom crowd in Billings, "and hit me right on the head in the middle of that eclipse, I knew I was destined for something big! Something big! And guess what? Five months later I invented *The Farming Game!*" As I sat down, the crowd roared with laughter.

13

1-800-222-GAME

• • • • • • • • • • • • • • • • • •

With the combined efforts of the Fox brothers and ourselves, by the end of our third Christmas season we had sold more than 100,000 games. But despite a heroic effort by Dick Fox, game sales had not come anywhere close to projections. Times were just too tough. Suicides by farmers were at an all-time high as the economic downturn, kicked into high gear by Carter's grain embargo and record-breaking drought, developed into a full-blown agricultural depression. While the dreams of thousands of farm families were crushed every week, the toll was the highest in Fox's prime marketplace, the Midwest.

Dick also had troubles that went far beyond trying to sell *The Farming Game*. He was also going through a divorce, and the family farms he managed were waging a survival battle of their own. After much agony, the Fox brothers decided that perhaps they weren't the ones to take *The Farming Game* over the top and relinquished their territory.

However, *The Farming Game* racked up an impressive list of accomplishments and a solid sales track record in the stores which had bought it. A big problem, though, was that we had never been able to get on the shelf in any of the large, nationwide chains to really test the mass market. Our game was being used in schools and universities all over the country, due to the game's accurate depiction of the family farm economy as seen from ground zero. In middle and high schools, the game was used in social studies, economics, and vocational-agriculture programs. At the college level, *The Farming Game* was used as an economic model, a skeleton on which instructors could hang tax structures, accounting systems, and various kinds of government interference. *The Farming Game* became an official course material of the "Ag In The Classroom" Program, run as a pilot program in San Francisco by the California Farm Bureau.

As the agricultural depression deepened, the continuing saga of the disintegration of life in rural America played on. The North Dakota State Mental Health Service started a program to deal with stress for farmers that was replicated across the Midwest. Farm families for the first time, tried a group counseling approach to deal with dismal private problems, bankruptcy, the loss of their homes, and their way of life. *The Farming Game* was used in that program. When the formal day sessions were over and everyone had gone back to the motel, the counselors got out our game for the evening's entertainment. The game proved a good vehicle to let the individual management styles of husband/wife or father/son teams emerge. But most important, playing *The Farming Game* was a way to laugh at the troubles that were making real life on the American farm a living hell.

We received fan letters from more than fifty foreign countries, from Nigeria to Denmark, requesting copies of *The Farming Game*. Word of mouth was spreading our reputation far and wide. Just how wide I had no appreciation of until one day we got a call from the president of an organization in California called Aviation Ministry Fellowship. AMF was an association of pilots who fly missionaries to their callings all over the globe. The week before the man calling from California had played our game deep in the jungles of Borneo! He was convinced *The Farming Game* was a perfect little piece of home, a great batteryless recreation tool for missionaries stationed in the bush the world over. He ordered several hundred games.

Borneo! The thought of people playing *The Farming Game* in the backcountry of Borneo literally blew my mind. Only two-and-a-half years before, on a tractor seat in Klickitat County, Washington, as the sun was coming up, I was the only person on the planet who knew about the game, and now they were playing *The Farming Game* in Borneo! What a small place the planet had become.

California proved to be a fertile marketplace for our mail-order business. Along with our efforts to find shelf space for our game, we continued the direct-mail campaign begun with our first season. California's diversified agricultural economy supported several strong farm publications, and the response to *The Farming Game* ads we placed in them was excellent. Along with game orders, the ads brought us contacts, people who were interested in raising the public consciousness about farming.

Carolyn Leavens, President of California Women for Agriculture (CWA), was particularly impressed with our game's ability to get the story of agriculture across to our urban cousins. She invited us to come and exhibit our game at a show that CWA was putting on at Fort Mason in San Francisco midsummer. The show was to be a first try, in a new format, to bridge the communication gap between farm and city. California agriculture was in the throes of the Medfly crisis when the CWA show came together. The Medfly threatened a huge range of crops, everything from tomatoes to citrus. The huge and lucrative export market for lemons, grapefruit and oranges to the Orient was thrown into disarray. Japan put up an immediate quarantine on fruit that came from any California county with even one Medfly sighting.

Fort Mason, the scheduled site for the CWA farm-city show, was an old World War Two military installation transformed into an urban park of sorts. The main structure of the park was a huge warehouse, several acres in size, sitting on a pier jutting into the bay. The CWA show was to be held in the vast warehouse.

I had an uncle who was a college professor living just south of the San Francisco airport. We arranged to stay with him during the show. Ann and I planned to leave our kids with my cousin so we could work the show together. When we arrived at my uncle's condo, we found my cousin ill, with headaches, nausea, and general malaise. She blamed it on the Medfly spraying.

I couldn't believe my ears. I explained to her that the cat she held in her lap with the flea and tick collar was exposing her to a far higher dose of chemicals than Medfly spraying.

"Oh no," she protested, "I haven't felt well since the spraying started!"

She was completely convinced she was sick from the deadly spray. In one last-ditch attempt to make my point, I asked her how, living next to the San Mateo Bridge with eight lanes of traffic, and Highway 101 with ten lanes of bumper-to-bumper cars and trucks, and also under an approach to SFO airport, how her body could be attuned to sense the addition of a miniscule amount of Malathion to the air already fouled with such huge quantities of so many other airborne chemicals? There was no doubt about it: bringing the farm message to San Francisco was going to be no easy task.

The CWA show was a huge success. It was heavily attended by the public and well covered in the San Francisco press. California Women for Agriculture, an umbrella group of women from every sector of California agriculture, did a great job of getting their points across. The warehouse at Fort Mason was packed by displays and exhibits from every phase of the most diverse agricultural state in the nation. The real crowd pleaser, and a big draw to the no-admission fair, was a huge farmers' market. It was a farmers' market like Francisco had never seen — with farmers selling their produce at the prices they received down at the farm! There were tons of avocados, kiwis, walnuts, peaches, apples, tomatoes, lettuce, dates, water-melons, and every other kind of vegetable and fruit imagin-able for sale, by the pound, at the per-ton farm gate prices. Every consumer purchase was an unbelievable bargain.

The CWA organizers had planned the layout of the show to require the public to walk all the way through the exhibit hall containing our information booths and displays, to reach the cornucopia of produce bargains. The booths came from every conceivable niche in agriculture. The sheep producers' booth held poster-size, color photo sequences of lovable coyotes lunching on lamb chops out on the open range. The tomato producers had a huge display warning the consumer not to put their tomatoes in the flavor-robbing refrigerator. Their advice was to store tomatoes at room temperature to build up the limited flavor of the new indestructible varieties of tomatoes. We were inspired by the energy and industry with which the women of CWA worked.

The produce section, as predicted, became a feeding frenzy of bargain-priced food shopping: artichokes at eight cents each, carrots at forty-six cents a ten-pound sack, lettuce at eleven cents a head. At each produce-vending counter, there was a display that showed the supermarket costs of the foods that were being offered. The chart broke the prices down, subtracting the store's margin, the broker's margin, the trucking costs, inspection, and all the other costs, finally arriving at the real cost per pound that went to the farmer, who made the whole thing possible.

The Fort Mason pier reached out into San Francisco Bay about a quarter of a mile. The produce section, located at the far end on the pier, required the bargain-shopping urbanites to carry their goodies a considerable distance back to their cars. The prices were so low in comparison to what people were used to paying that virtually every shopper bought as much of their favorite foods as they could possibly haul away. *The Farming Game* booth was near an outside aisle of the show, so during the moments when we weren't too busy, we watched an unending stream of people loaded down, heading back to their cars dragging large produce boxes filled to the brim with goodies. The quantities of produce some people were trying to move were unbelievable. Their eyes had definitely been bigger than their muscles, most stopping to rest every few yards. After the shoppers made the quarter-mile to the front of the building, they still had a long way to go. We farm people, manning the booths, got a perverse kick watching the struggling parade of produce packers go by. It was the first time many of those urban shoppers had ever really worked for their food, and we couldn't help but enjoy seeing them sweating a little for something so essential, and yet, in America, so taken for granted.

The show was very successful for us. We made a number of good friends and lots of valuable contacts. We sold just as many games to the other farmers at the show as we sold to the public. We found that *The Farming Game* had a solid reputation already built with the farm folks who ran the show but who never saw our game in stores before.

As Ann and I drove north on the way back to the Breaks Ranch from San Francisco, we debated our next course of action with the business.

With the Foxes out of the picture and the whole country to go after, we decided to hire a full-time sales manager. We needed help in getting *The Farming Game* into stores to allow us to tap the huge potential we believed our game possessed. *The Farming Game* might be the best idea since sliced bread, but if we couldn't get it on the shelves, how would anybody know? A sales manager was the only answer. We needed a person who could devote all his energy to selling our product. It was early summer, so we still had time for an aggressive sales campaign for the upcoming Christmas season, if we got a sales manager on board and quickly.

Selling *The Farming Game* to the retail trade had proved quite a challenge. One-product companies, like The Weekend Farmer Company, have a hard time even getting in to see a big chain store buyer. Ann's function in our company was taking care of the office, from finances to shipping. My job was production, promotion, and sales, and I desperately wanted someone else to take over sales. With five billion potential *Farming Game* customers in the world, the job was far bigger than I was, and I would readily admit it. Besides, I kept repeating to myself, I invented the game to save the family farm, not to become a salesman.

In 1979, when the game was introduced, we were swimming upstream in the marketplace with a game that was nearly twice as big and twice as costly as the cardboard competition. *The Farming Game* had been built to our standards, not those of the marketplace. In 1980, the video-game fad was in full swing. The explosive growth in the electronic games had sent shock waves through the toy industry. The trade journals predicted that cardboard games like ours would become a thing of the past. Store buyers had been very cautious about taking on a product from a "dying" product category, especially one not manufactured by the majors. To top it all off, the whole subject of farming had become so downright depressing to the general public, inundated with the constant reminders of the agricultural depression and farm bankruptcies on the nightly news, that the subject matter of our game became a tough sell.

Agriculture, in many people's minds, had become like AIDS: farming, the terminal economic disease. Yet despite all these obstacles, Ann and I continued to sell tens of thousands of copies of *The Farming Game*. J.C. Penney came within inches of stocking our game, but days before we were to ship their first order, the buyer who liked our product was replaced by one who didn't. Surely, Ann and I thought, if we had the right person working for us selling *The Farming Game* full time, we might finally break into the big time.

Running a manufacturing and distribution business from a ranch fifteen miles of bad road from town presented many challenges. Finding a qualified and energetic candidate for the position in our unlikely location was also proving a difficult task. There were many people looking for work, since the winds of change in rural America had cut many people loose from their former occupations.

Goldendale's International Tractor dealer had gone out of business. An International dealership out of Oregon was testing the waters in Goldendale by putting a full-time equipment salesman in our community. Pat Powell, an ex-farm boy, tried his best to make the equipment dealer's experiment a success. In the early seventies Goldendale had been a farm town which supported three tractor dealerships but was soon to have none as the John Deere dealership also closed its doors for good.

Try as he might, Pat was not making much headway selling equipment in the Goldendale area. After Pat stopped by the ranch on a sales call, I got to thinking that he might be a potential sales manager candidate. Ann had met his wife in town and found her to be energetic and enthusiastic. When we broached the subject to Pat he jumped at the chance. Big Red's Goldendale expansion project was not going well; Pat and his wife Kathy saw the handwriting on the wall. They were looking for new opportunities. Kathy was weighted down with three small children but was willing to help out too, as a shipping clerk, office girl, or in whatever capacity we needed.

We were preparing to print the sixth edition of *The Farming Game*. We fine tuned the game slightly with each new edition to reflect the changing nature of farming. We added: Carter's Grain Embargo; a natural disaster, Mount St. Helens Ash on Your Hay; the Apple Maggot Fly (cousin to the dreaded Medfly), Doubled Interest Rates, and other fun small changes. As the government started to respond to the disaster they had helped cause, I soon realized that if I wanted to keep our game current, I was going to have to start adding federal subsidies and the government control that comes along with those checks. Ann and I decided we wanted to keep *The Farming Game* a picture of a free-market farm economy and vowed that we were done tinkering with our game.

With our efforts and the press coverage we sold 150,000 games without ever being on the shelves of any major chains. Ann and I reasoned if we hired our sales manager on a salary with a volume incentive as a bonus, we would get the extra effort needed to get *The Farming Game* in stores all over the country. And if we could do that, our financial worries on the Breaks Ranch would be over for good.

Pat signed on as our sales manager, giving the tractor dealer his two weeks' notice. By adding Pat and a woman from Klickitat to help Ann in the office, we increased our ability to get work done, but we also increased our responsibilities of having to manage employees, something new for our small family operation. Training Pat to channel his efforts in the areas we already identified proved far more time consuming than we anticipated. Ann and I would spend a several-hour session brainstorming with Pat and think we had achieved a consensus on a course of action. But after he went home and discussed those ideas with his wife, he would come back to work the next day moving in a different direction. Kathy gave him some good input, but we would have to spend another jaw session with Pat to get back to where we'd left off the day before. Kathy soon was so full of ideas about *The Farming Game* she was about ready to pop! She'd given up a career to have their three kids, and after five years of diapers and baby talk, she was starving for stimulation and just couldn't stay out of it.

Good farmers learn that, rather than fighting nature, it is sometimes better to go with the flow. We decided to go with the flow and hire Kathy too. But we didn't need another cook in the kitchen trying to figure out how to sell more copies of the game. We put Kathy's supply of pent-up energy to work as our press agent, our own in-house PR department. I had been successful in getting media coverage, just by showing up at newspapers and radio stations wherever I traveled. The story of what Ann and I were doing, why we were doing it, and how we were doing it made interesting news copy. We planned a press tour for the three-state area. Our sales strategy was to combine Pat's efforts working the stores while I worked the media.

We timed my press tour for early November. Our goal was to work all the major media outlets from Boise to Seattle. Kathy attacked her job as PR coordinator with a vengeance. When the dust settled, she ran me through a grinder of fifty-six interviews in twenty-five days. I was accustomed to talking to the press long before this workout, but Kathy had set up so many interviews in such quick succession that, by the end of the month, I felt like a punch-drunk fighter reeling from too many questions.

Most of the interviews were newspaper or radio, but Kathy landed several TV spots as well. After several in-station interviews on talk shows, Kathy convinced a producer that *The Farming Game* would make a good story for a Portland TV magazine show called *Faces and Places.*

Pat, unfortunately, was not making nearly as much headway in placing our game in stores as Kathy was in promoting it to the media. We wanted to be on the shelf across the region when the media blitz was in full swing so we could prove to the skeptical store buyers that, if it ever got on the shelf, *The Farming Game* could be a big seller.

The day the *Faces and Places* TV crew from Portland drove out to the Breaks Ranch was a typical, overcast, early-winter day. The Columbia Gorge was rainy as usual; the first ice and snows of the year had not yet arrived. I liked to have interviewers from the city come to the ranch. Coming from Goldendale, our road, though rough, was passable. Traveling from Portland, the only approach was the old state highway, which was built before statehood and had not changed much since the wagons rolled over it. The bed of the road was not quite two vehicles wide. If two vehicles met, one of them had to back up to a spot wide enough to allow the other vehicle to pass. City dwellers used to the blacktop, rush-hour freeways found our two-mile-long back road, with its 800-foot vertical dropoff and no guardrails, quite unnerving. I figured if an interviewer arrived at the top of the hill at our place with his knees knocking, I would have no problem getting his full attention.

About ten minutes after the TV crew from Portland showed up at the ranch, it started to snow and in no time at all we were in the midst of a regular Breaks Ranch blizzard. The falling snow made a great backdrop for the scenes they shot of me feeding the cows and loading hay on the pickup at the barn. In the three hours it took to complete the filming, which would air in a segment only about three to five minutes long, it snowed about a foot. I could feel the anxiety building among the crew as they packed their gear away. They seemed to be contemplating the trip back down the grade in the studio van. The snow had definitely turned the grade into a four-wheel-drive passage only. After the camera crew was loaded into the van, I mentioned to the driver that there was another, safer, way out of the Breaks Ranch than the way they'd come. The crew let out a sigh of relief so loud, it sounded like one of the tires had sprung a leak.

Winter progressed, and *The Farming Game* put another Christmas season behind it. Pat and Kathy's combined efforts had definitely made a difference in our sales figures. The challenge was to balance their contributions against the increased overhead. The next big Christmas sales season was almost ten months away.

In our farming operation, we had always done everything we could to avoid full-time employees and all the headaches and responsibilities they brought with them. Ann and I debated the problem for weeks, until we saw the results of a sales trip Pat took to the Chicago Gift Fair. The 4,000-mile road trip cost far more than it brought in. Having a salesman on the road with a one-product line was looking less and less wise. Kathy was without a task now that our media blitz was over and was itching to move her family to Portland, where she might find more interesting work. Ann and I decided it was best to call off the sales manager experiment and let Pat go.

We decided that sales reps who charged a twelve to fifteen percent commission for handling gift lines appeared to be our solution. The nice thing about sales reps working on straight commission was that they don't come with employee management headaches; and also, if they didn't sell games, they didn't get paid. We also decided to update our mail-order business by installing an 800 number. At that time, 800 numbers were in their infancy, so we practically had our choice of number and letter combinations. We chose 800-222-GAME, and we printed the number on the next run of game boxes right next to our address.

While the growing mail-order and wholesale business kept Ann and her office gal occupied, I took to the highways for another season of farm shows. I booked booth space for several shows in the fall, after my summer's farming was finished. Life on the road was upgraded with the purchase of a near-new Dodge fifteen-passenger van that, when stripped of its seats, carried enough copies of *The Farming Game* to equal the same gross dollar value as five thirty-ton semi loads of alfalfa hay. The van, with its big hauling capacity, also allowed me to take longer road trips.

In late September, as I was preparing to go on my first road trip, I thought it would be fun to take the family out the night before I left. My widowed mother had moved to The Dalles to be near her only set of grandkids and to finish the last years of her career as an RN at the hospital there. Ann and I decided we'd call Grandma and take her out for dinner. The kids wanted pizza.

The dinner conversation that night at Dave's Hometown Pizza centered around the Rajneeshees, a religious sect, and their takeover of the town of Antelope, and their play to take over Wasco County politics. Several years before, the Bhagwan Shree Rajneesh, with his sixty-five Rolls Royces and hordes of red-garbed followers, had descended on a 65,000-acre ranch they'd purchased near the little town of Antelope.

The hundred-square-mile ranch was so large it spanned three counties. The ranch headquarters and the location of their instant city of the future, Rajneeshpuram, was in Wasco County, with The Dalles as county seat. The Rajneeshees had candidates filed for virtually every slot from sheriff to assessor in the upcoming primary elections. The locals were worried about the potential block-voting power of the thousands of the Bhagwan's devotees and a huge pool of homeless people the Rajneeshees were importing from cities all across the country. Buses full of the homeless arrived hourly in the red city in the middle of nowhere. The Rajneeshees had mounted a full-scale effort to swamp the ballot box with votes for their own candidates.

The turmoil that had accompanied the Bhagwan's attempt to set up his Oregon commune and build his city of enlightenment had spawned a Gorge-wide rumor mill that hatched some juicy whoppers. The current rumor was that the Rajneeshees were trying to poison the population of The Dalles, to make them too sick to go to the polls and vote on election day. That afternoon, my mother had several deathly-ill patients in her ward at The Dalles Hospital, all diagnosed with salmonella poisoning.

As I returned to the salad bar for a second helping, I couldn't help but laugh at the idea that the Rajneeshees were behind the salmonella outbreak. But what could one expect from a rural community which had been whipped into a lather by the radical actions of the Bhagwan and his followers? Their lawsuits and legal actions had turned the Wasco County court system into a quagmire. Their newest scheme, not nearly so far-fetched as poisoning Wasco County, was trucking in the homeless before election day to take advantage of Oregon's twenty-four-hour waiting period between registering to vote and being eligible to do so. Though the Bhagwan had taken a vow of silence, in his place Ma Anand Sheela, his lieutenant, blistered the national airwaves with abusive statements about the racist treatment her fellow devotees were receiving at the hands of the local Wasco County rednecks. In fact, during an interview on the *Phil Donahue Show,* Phil was forced to turn off her mike to shut up her scathing streams of profanity. The spillover from the Rajneeshee conflict had the whole Columbia Gorge region up in arms, as the fight for the Wasco County ballot box played out on the network evening news.

About midnight, a few hours after our pizza dinner with my mom, I woke up sick as hell. I spent the next several hours emptying the remnants of my dinner down the toilet. After the gastric attacks subsided, my temperature shot sky high — I had food poisoning. I was the only one of our family to get sick. But I was the only one in the family to eat the salad bar that night. For the next two days my guts rumbled and churned like a beast had been caught inside. I postponed my road trip a few more days until I could last more than an hour before making a mad dash to the john.

Several months later it was proven that the Rajneeshees had brewed up pathenogens out at their ranch and really had poisoned the salad bars in The Dalles as part of their failed Wasco County election takeover plot. Foul-mouthed Sheela and a number of her cronies were sent off to jail.

14

The Other
Washington

• • • • • • • • • • • • • • • • • •

The Farming Game's success had halted the backward slide of the Breaks Ranch into insolvency. The cattle market was still in a deep slump, but with the extra income from the game, we were able to buy the concrete and lumber needed to build a feedbarn to solve my winter feeding headaches. To build the barn we used poles salvaged from our old, undependable, overhead four-party phone line that snaked down the hill through the woods to house. The overhead line had been replaced by cable, installed to service our fast-growing telephone needs. When the cable hookup was complete, the phone company let me have the old line poles, wire and insulators for salvage. The new feedbarn was designed to store hay stacked with a balewagon, never once touched with bale hooks. Feeding the hay out would be as simple as cutting the wires and rolling a bale off the stack. We would no longer be at the mercy of the weather, trying to get our cows fed in the winter's snow and mud. Feeding cows at the new barn was now easy enough for the kids to do it.

Our game business, which had started in the living room, had spread and taken over our entire basement. To avoid the high cost of renting warehouse space in Portland, we bought two forty-foot semi-trailers. We hired our hay trucker to take them down to Goodwill in Portland to be filled with games and then hauled to the ranch. They were parked down in the barnyard as mobile storage units, holding 7,000 games apiece. I could then buck pickup loads of games a couple hundred at a time up to the house for shipment as they were needed. Our business was humming. UPS came five days a week, and as *The Farming Game* neared 175,000 copies sold, we started to look again to new horizons.

Many farmers were going broke, and everyone else was holding on for dear life. The agricultural depression had a devastating effect on Klickitat County land values. They crashed to half the level of just a few years before. We witnessed the drying up of the so-called "back-to-the-land movement" as the county's pilgrims starved out, one by one. Their empty little mini-ranches placed lots of property on the market. Ann and I started to look for more farmland to buy.

Our daughter Laura was followed by the birth of a third son, Philip. Life in our house, with *The Farming Game*s coming and going, the telephone ringing, and the kids growing, was hectic, to say the very least. Our home business had outgrown its headquarters. We found a small piece of property four miles closer to town that was up for sale. It had a shop building that seemed perfect to house *The Farming Game* office with plenty of space to warehouse the product.

The parcel near town we bought was the former head-quarters of a 900-acre ranch owned by California developers and subdivided into twenty-acre ranchettes. The plots were sold for $1,000 down and the balance paid on owner's contract at $100 a month. In the late seventies the buyers of the twenty-acre tracts were an endless stream of urbanites seeking rural refuge. Most of the parcels, in short order, turned into twenty-acre weed patches.

Moving our growing business out of our house was a godsend. We reoccupied large areas of the house that had been swallowed up by *The Farming Game* for years. The switch eliminated the many hours a week I spent as a warehouse man. No more having to move product from the semi-trailers to the shipping area and keeping the 150-foot sidewalks free of snow for handtrucking the games from the basement out to the UPS truck. In the new location, our UPS man just backed up to the warehouse door and loaded. With our 800 number, a $25,000 direct-mail advertising budget, continued road trips, and lots of word-of-mouth referral orders, the activity kept Ann's two-person office bustling.

We were pleased to discover that during the Christmas season of 1984, *Trivial Pursuit* sold millions of copies at $35 each in the mass market. That new game completely changed perceptions of what the public would pay for a boardgame. As a result, the buyers no longer flinched at the price we charged for our big, high-quality product.

Our wholesale business had grown to 600 accounts, which required computerization to keep efficient track of the billings. Home computers were in their infancy. We had already seen two systems we purchased turn obsolete in as many years. Sales reps and distributors did a reasonably good job of filling the void created when Pat left, but we still had not broken into the shelves of any major national chain yet.

I was searching for something to make it happen, something to give us a boost, something to give us the exposure to put us over the top. I didn't have a clue as to what to do next, when out of the blue I got a call from an old friend. Carolyn Leavens, the leader of California Women for Agriculture. She had just been elected to the post of President of American Agri-Women, the umbrella group that represented farm women from every sector of agriculture. Carolyn called to say that she had been invited to speak in Pasco, Washington, at an agriculture convention and wanted to know if we lived near enough for a visit.

Carolyn flew into the Portland airport, where I picked her up after a side trip to Goodwill to check on game production. National agriculture was lucky to have such an attractive, articulate, and savvy spokeswoman. Carolyn and her husband grew citrus fruit in Ventura County, California. She grew up on a wheat ranch in Central Washington and was glad to be coming "home" for a short visit.

The demands of her presidency of California Women for Agriculture, were intense, but nothing like the responsibility she assumed with the presidency of American Agri-Women. In fact the demands of the job at a time when agriculture was in its darkest days since the Great Depression was beyond intense. Carolyn had a travel schedule that would make even a flight attendant blanch.

Carolyn said she came up with an idea for a media event to increase the coverage of the 1985 annual Farm Women's Forum sponsored by the Department of Agriculture in Washington, D.C. She explained that farm women from all the fifty states would attend the Forum, whose sole objective was to have farm folks converge on the nation's capital to provide their elected officials a reality check. Farm women were the backbone of the business end of agriculture, usually keeping the books of the nation's largest industry.

Like no other time in the past fifty years, the prevailing economic conditions forced America's traditionally independent farmers to get more involved collectively. It was that, or die separately. The tractorcades of the late seventies were the first statement by rural America that things were going wrong, that a crash was under way. The protests had gotten the farmers public attention, and not all of it good either. Some parts of the story played in the press in negative ways. The protests created many different impressions than the tractorcade organizers had intended in the first place. But in this crisis we had to do something, even if it was wrong.

Carolyn Leavens' primary job as president of AAW was to create public exposure of the plight of agriculture in the mid-eighties. She worked to correct misconceptions in the media and frequently acted as a spokesperson for the whole of agriculture at public hearings. Farm Women's Forum was a relatively new offering by the Department of Agriculture. It was an effort by the Department to provide a format for direct communication between the policy makers in that "other" Washington and the people affected by those policies.

The Forum was also an opportunity for alerting the press about agriculture and its concerns. Carolyn, and other leaders in agriculture, were finding it increasingly hard to catch the public ear. The news from rural America had been so dismal for so long that the media quickly grew callous to the tragedy that stalked farm country. Family farms held for generations were on the auction block; small-town banks and businesses were folding by the thousands. The fabric of American rural life was unraveling, and with it the wellsprings of the American character. But this was old news.

To meet this challenge, Carolyn came up with a creative plan to try to tell agriculture's story. She thought that while they attended the upcoming conference, American Agri-Women should distribute a copy of *The Farming Game* to every member of Congress! AAW would use the distribution as a media event to create exposure during the Farm Women's Forum. *The Farming Game*'s use in the Ag in the Classroom program, its exposure in over a thousand schools nationwide, and the academic reviews verifying the accuracy of the picture that our game painted, gave *The Farming Game* the credibility to carry a serious message to the halls of Congress. The fact that the message was an entertaining kick in the butt was just so much the better. The standard ways of getting attention, in coverage-hungry Washington, D.C., was not working for farmers anymore. Carolyn hoped this fresh approach would both get attention and add something useful to the national dialogue.

Ann and I liked the idea immediately. It was bold, it was unusual, and it stood a fair chance of creating lots of exposure, especially if nothing else major happened on the Hill on presentation day. Using *The Farming Game* to spread agriculture's message might just be odd enough on a dead news day to get major network news coverage.

By the time Carolyn left to continue her speaking tour, Ann and I committed to donate *The Farming Game*s required for her effort. My head reeled with the possibilities. This could be our big chance to get national coverage. This could be our big chance for the exposure that would help us finally break down the resistance of the buyers for the big national chains who had ignored our product far too long.

But this opportunity was about more than just commerce. I invented the game to say something about the underrecognized links between the the two percent of us who farm, and the other 98 percent who eat. The great famines that had decimated the populations of Europe in the 1800s were unknown in the U.S. American agriculture h was so productive and efficient that we few remaining farmers had freed virtually the entire population of our country to do other work, to provide society with luxury items, like cars, furniture, or chewing gum. Farmers produced the essentials for life, and for a continually shrinking slice of national gross income. Huge surpluses of food, produced beyond our own national needs, were exported in quantities sufficient to pay the bill for all the oil imported into the U.S.A..

Common sense dictates that if you have a brain tumor, you see a brain surgeon. My small interview experience had made it obvious to me that if we wanted to get media coverage in D.C., we needed to hire a public relations firm. Washington, D.C. was a churning pool of special interests, seeking attention from the city's thousands of media people. Without professional management, *The Farming Game* would surely be lost in the shuffle.

If *The Farming Game* press conference, which kicked off the game presentation to Congress, was on a midweek day without other competing world-breaking crises, there was a fair chance that the major media might find our story offbeat enough for extensive coverage. It was a once-in-a-lifetime opportunity which, if we played it right, could make *The Farming Game* a household word instantly. I was convinced that hiring a professional PR firm was the only way to ensure a successful media blitz in D.C., and I soon convinced Ann of it, too. We hoped the sales from the potential exposure would be worth the big expense of putting it all together. After Ann gave me her reluctant okay to spend the money, I started a search for the right firm.

We hired Ketchum and Associates, one of the big ten PR firms. Ketchum handled many clients with agricultural interests. Before I knew it, I had my own account executive and a contract obligating us for ten thousand bucks. The amount did not scare me, as we had an advertising budget almost three times that much for our mail-order business. In fact, if our efforts were successful, and we garnered the coverage we needed from the event, the $10,000 Ketchum wanted could be the cheapest advertising buy in history.

The date of the Farm Women's Forum was in late April, and six weeks ahead of time Ann and I flew to Washington, D.C., to meet the people at Ketchum. We wanted to meet our account executive in person before we signed the $10,000 contract. If we were spending that much money on hot air, we wanted to see the source beforehand. A face-to-face visit with our PR people also would be a good opportunity to give them a training session on the marvelous qualities of our game. Hell, for $10,000 we should be able to turn our PR man into a full-fledged *Farming Game* fanatic for a few weeks.

The cab ride from the airport to our downtown hotel was a culture shock. Our driver was from Zaire. He drove his seedy cab like a madman in the heavy traffic. We breathed a sigh of relief when he dropped us off in front of the hotel. It was now twenty years since I lived in the East. Standing on the sidewalk in front of our hotel, I felt as out of place as a fish on the dock. My countrified eyes could hardly believe what they were seeing. Limos passed by every few seconds. We were so far out of our league here that it wasn't even funny. As I savored the foul urban air on the street, I knew down deep inside that hiring a PR firm had been the right thing to do.

The six-week countdown to *The Farming Game* Congressional presentation day whirled away at a blinding speed. I was on the phone so much I started to develop a cauliflower ear. I called everyone I knew, looking for anybody who might have an in at our nation's capital. As it turned out, to my unbelievable luck, one of my best friends had been a college roommate of the news director at a big-three TV affiliate in Washington, D.C. Based on that introduction, I had the ear of one of the most influential men in a sea of influential men. The news director was down-home and friendly as hell over the phone, from a small town in Wisconsin and saw nothing wrong in educating the halls of Congress with *The Farming Game*. He promised, barring any major conflicting story, that his station would cover our press conference! We had finally uncovered the direct line to national network coverage.

Our Congressman, Rep. Sid Morrison, an apple grower from the Yakima Valley, was an early fan of *The Farming Game*. He enthusiastically offered to support our efforts in every way possible to make the press event a success. Sid volunteered to help recruit a few of his colleagues to attend the kick-off press conference and offered the use of his office as the distribution point. Sid had worked with Carolyn Leavens many times before on agriculture-related legislation, and held her in highest regard. Our combined efforts gave us a good chance of getting the big coverage we were seeking. The calendar of competing events for the distribution day continued to look fairly blank, and as the time got closer, my hopes that we were on the verge of becoming a household word increased almost daily.

My mother-in-law, Betty, was planning to be in the East at the same time for a board meeting at Stratford Hall Plantation in tidewater Virginia, the ancestral home of Robert E. Lee. Betty suggested a cheaper alternative than staying in a hotel. She suggested that we stay with her at the Solgrave Club on Du Pont Circle. Betty was a member of the Sunset Club in Seattle, and the two clubs had reciprocal lodging agreements. I didn't find the idea of staying at a stuffy women's club appealing; that is, until I heard the room was half the price of a downtown hotel room.

I went to Olympia, our state capital, to see what support I could find to make our operation in Washington, D.C., more successful. I met with both our representatives, our state senator, the Chair of the House Agriculture committee, and the State Secretary of Agriculture to appraise them all of our efforts to act as agricultural missionaries from the "other" Washington to the power brokers in D.C.

I found support everywhere. To my complete surprise a week later, I was notified that the Senate and the House of Representatives had passed Floor Resolution 85-65 supporting our contributions to public education and the stability of the American family farm.

Getting support in Olympia had been so easy that my expectations for a grand success in Washington grew by the day. Nick, our account executive at Ketchum, arranged about two dozen interviews for me during the three days preceding the kickoff press conference. Our media effort was a long shot, a $10,000 gamble, but so was the invention and marketing of our game!

Agriculture is the nation's largest and most diverse industry, the bedrock on which the American dream has been built. As the farming population has shrunk to between

1 percent and 2 percent of the national population, it has been easy for the larger society to ignore concerns vital to survival of the American family farm. Modern life no longer seems to depend on the the soil and the turn of the seasons. *The Farming Game* was more than just another toy. Our game wasn't Trivial Pursuit; it was the essential pursuit! I hoped, in my own small way, to contribute something useful to the national dialogue with *The Farming Game*.

Ten days from D-Day, I started to contact the Northwest media, from the weekly newspapers to the TV stations in Portland. The reception I was getting was overwhelmingly positive. Virtually all the media people I contacted indicated they would cover the story. I called the editor of the *Yakima Herald Republic* to appraise him of the upcoming events, and offer an idea I had for his paper. My idea was that, while I was on this quixotic quest to Camelot, I would write a series of two or three columns on a farmer's view of the goings-on in the other Washington, our capital. The style would be a tongue-in-cheek look at the seat of government, as Mr. Dirt Farmer goes to Washington, D.C. The editor was enthusiastic; he said he would love to see the columns and commented that Will Rogers had shown humor was sometimes the only way to make sense of the activities in our nation's capital.

Ann and I arrived in Washington all primed for the big event. Our third-floor accommodations at the Solgrave Club were unpretentious, an elegance way past its prime. There was only a handful of guest rooms at the club which maintained a dining room for Washington's elite. The club was primarily a collection of sumptuous and chandeliered ballrooms used by the members for receptions and entertaining the rich and powerful. The stately building occupied its own pie-shaped city block within the radius of Du Pont

Circle, in a neighborhood populated by obscure embassies and townhouses. I had never before stayed in a place like the Solgrave Club; and having arrived just fresh off the ranch, where the day before we had branded and castrated our calves, I felt on foreign soil.

Almost immediately Monday afternoon, PR Nick put me to work. The AAW kick-off press conference was to be at nine a.m. on Thursday. Nick had me scheduled nonstop for interviews with radio commentators and chain newspapers all day Tuesday and Wednesday. By the time I got rolling on my second interview, I was no longer nervous. The interviewers in Washington, D.C., were no different than their counterparts in the hinterlands I dealt with before. Washington was going to be a piece of cake.

The weather was unseasonally warm for late April, with temperatures in the nineties. The heat and humidity took the sharp creases out of my new, dark blue suit. We scurried from interview to interview in a succession of funky taxis driven by a dizzying array of foreigners. With twenty-four hours to go before the press conference, the Capitol events calendar still looked mercifully vacant. The news director of the network affiliate who promised news coverage reassured me that if nothing else big was happening, our press conference was on as scheduled for Thursday morning.

The American Agri-Women's press conference was to be held in a Senate Anteroom. Bob Dole, the senator from the great agricultural state of Kansas and the Senate Majority Leader, promised to attend. He would receive the first of the games from AAW President Carolyn Leavens. My dreams were within hours of coming true! Ann and I retired to our rooms early to store energy for the next day's long-awaited event, skipping out on Carolyn's *Farming*

Game presentation to the Secretary of Agriculture at a Farm Women's Forum legislative reception that evening.

The window air-conditioner in our rented room had given up the ghost while we were out that day. I sat on the end of my bed in the stifling East Coast heat, shower water dripping on the rug in front of me, watching to the evening news. The Senate had just announced that it would hold its first press conference of the legislative session on the budget the following morning. The news report zapped me like a cattle prod! The budget whale had just landed in the bathtub with us. The opening shots in the annual political battle over money were set to be fired on the same day that Agri-Women had set for their press conference!

I received more disappointing news early Thursday morning when, at breakfast, Ann and I met with Carolyn and a few of the other women helping with the distribution of the games in the halls of Congress. It seemed that Wednesday night at the reception given by the Department of Agriculture for the Farm Women's Forum, farm women from all fifty states and every sector of agriculture were on hand. The reception's purpose was to meet with legislators on an informal basis, yet only two out of the 535 legislators in Congress had attended! Carolyn was livid. It was unbelievable that only two representatives had bothered to show up to meet with farm women from every state in the union. Congress had slighted the very people who represented the backbone of the nation's biggest industry! My congressman, Sid Morrison, and Carolyn's congressman were the only legislators who showed. They had to appear because they were on the program for presenting the Secretary of Agriculture with his copy of *The Farming Game*.

Carolyn was bitter. She said, "If that reception had been for the heads of the banking industry, the steel industry, the automobile industry, or some tinhorn dictator at his flashy embassy, there would have been at least a dozen congressmen in attendance. We are the biggest plus in our nation's balance of trade, with more total capital assets than the Fortune 500 companies, and we can't even get their attention during the worst times for farmers since the Depression."

Congressman Morrison, who walked us over to the Capitol Building for our scheduled press conference, tried to soften the bad news he had to relay: the major Senate press conference kicking off the budget battles was scheduled for fifteen minutes following our own. In all likelihood, all the major media reps who scheduled to cover our press conference would reprioritize and set up to cover the budget hassle instead.

After the piece I'd seen on the evening news about the upcoming budget skirmish, I had lain awake all night in our sweltering room at the Solgrave Club worrying about just such an outcome. Who could blame the news directors for making that choice? After all, farm woes were old news; the public had seen enough of the walking wounded from America's farms and ranches. In contrast, the beginnings of the budget fight had all the color and excitement of tag-team wrestling.

Senate Majority Leader Dole whizzed through our press conference on his way to the budget press conference down the hall. From start to finish, the American Agri-Women's press conference was over in twenty minutes. The press conference was not a total disaster; it was surprisingly well covered, considering our competition, but it wasn't the monster success I had hoped. I had dreamed of attracting the attention of the whole nation for just a few celebrated minutes, but instead got only a tiny share.

The distribution of *The Farming Game* to the offices in the House and Senate office buildings went smoothly in the hands of the hardworking farm women. Some returned to our central distribution point at Sid Morrison's office with funny tales of the reception they got delivering our games. I gave a few more interviews while the last copies were distributed. And then it was completely over.

Ann and I walked arm in arm down the halls of the Sam Rayburn Office Building, basking in the realization that the pressure was over and, for better or worse, our Washington, D.C., adventure was complete.

Ann stopped me mid-stride and, looking me in the eye, said, "You shouldn't be the least bit disappointed with yourself for how this turned out. You did everything you possibly could. Just look where we are; look at what we accomplished."

A big smile broke out on her face. "And after all," she said, "it is only just a game!" With that, Ann threw her arms around my neck and kissed me for all she was worth.

Afterword

After Washington, D.C., and seven years of all-consuming devotion, Ann and I both needed a break from the business of selling *The Farming Game*. I jumped ship first, leaving the sales and promotion of the game to fend for itself. Starting a year or two after the game's invention, I devoted increasingly larger amounts of my time to public involvement, serving on numerous local boards, and wound up being appointed to the Washington State Senate in 1988 to fill a vacant seat. I lost the election to retain my seat in a recount by only 166 votes out of the 32,000 cast. That loss, as painful as it was at the time, in retrospect, was one of the luckiest things that ever happened to me as a husband and father.

Ann had better luck at the polls than I, and won her own election to the local school board. She became the office manager of our county fair and also went back to college. Eventually, she became the superintendent of our rural school district. During this time, Ann, who hadn't dropped her responsibilities like I had, somehow, on top of all her other activities, continued to run the game business too. The game sold nearly 200,000 additional copies in this period with very little help from me.

One afternoon in the winter of 1994, a surprise phone call opened an exciting new chapter in the journey of the game that had begun on that tractor fifteen years before. It was an opportunity to play a tiny part in one of the most significant geopolitical events of the twentieth century, the revitalization of the Russian economy after the collapse of the USSR. The call was from Michael Harvey, an employee of the World Bank, who had just discovered *The Farming Game*. Michael's boss had him looking for tools to assist in the land privatization effort in the new Russia. After the disintegration of the former Soviet Union, the World Bank decided to assist Russia with social infrastructure gaps first before tackling the more standard World Bank type of investments like harbors, dams and factories. For private property and a market economy to take hold, the World Bank believed that Russia first needed many things, including laws to govern and protect land ownership, banking procedures that would allow commerce to happen, and ways to create knowledge and capitalist mind-set among Russia's newly private farmers and businessmen.

The afternoon he called me was Michael's last day in the States before flying to Moscow to go on station. He was lunching with a Seattle businessman. Over the meal he talked about his frustration in finding a good farm simulation teaching tool.

His businessman guest looked him in the eye and said, "What? You've never heard of *The Farming Game*?"

Michael said, "No."

"Well then, what are you doing for the rest of the afternoon?"

The businessman paid the check, took Michael home, and broke out his copy of the game. Three hours later Michael called me. He had found exactly the capitalist tool he was looking for. And five months later, at the World Bank's request, I too was on a plane headed for Moscow.

I had traveled out of the United States once before, to England with Ann on business, so I was surprised at the amount of nervous apprehension that was building up in the pit of my stomach as the British Airways plane made its final approach to Sheremetyevo, Moscow's international airport. The landing was soft and professional, and as we taxied in past an unending boneyard of passenger aircraft in various stages of dismantle out on the tarmac, I loosened my deathgrip on my seat's armrests. The strange cyrillic script on the sides of the planes was unmistakable evidence that we were truly in the land of hammer and sickle.

Images of my Cold War childhood came flooding back like long-forgotten nightmares. Before my eyes, my long-dead father reappeared. It was in our family dining room at the house in Princeton, New Jersey. I was thirteen years old. Before dinner Dad had gotten us kids to sit down at the table to tell us something he said was very, very important.

"Today President Kennedy gave Russian Premier Khrushchev an ultimatum. Get your missile bases out of Cuba, or else!" my dad explained. "And if the Russians don't back down, tomorrow at this time we could be in the middle of World War Three."

As the message sank into me like a giant weight, my little brothers and sisters fought and squirmed in their seats. Mom was crying quietly out in the kitchen.

"War with Russia means nuclear bombs," he began again. "It means mass death and destruction on a scale never before seen by mankind in all of human history. It might possibly mean that tomorrow at this time we could all be dead." He removed his glasses and wiped his eyes.

I snapped back to reality as my plane lurched to a stop at the gate.

The cold passageway led us passengers down a series of stairs to the basement of the airport. The hurry and bustle of the passengers came to a dead standstill at the bottom of those stairs. Russian soldiers with submachine guns were every-where. Ahead of us were a dozen or so lines for passport and visa inspection. Inside glass booths, under the glow of high illumination, soldiers meticulously studied the papers of each and every traveler. They used blacklights and large, powerful magnifying glasses to inspect the documents, often making calls to their superiors before finally stamping the visas and returning the papers to the waiting travelers. They then started the process anew with the next passenger. As I inched forward toward my turn at the inquisition, I broke out in a cold sweat, half wanting to run back up the jetway and reboard the plane for the free world.

The ride into Moscow with two World Bank people who were also on my plane and all our luggage packed into the Lada, a tiny Fiat-sized Russian car, was close, to say the least. The highway into the city was crowded big trucks. On the outskirts of Moscow were mile after mile of huge, naked, depressing apartment buildings in varying states of construction or decay. Entering the city proper, the traffic increased fivefold. As the radio blared strange music and the driver and the World Bank people conversed in Russian, my head was swimming with jet lag and cultural overload.

....

The World Bank put me up where they always stayed: at the $350 per night Metropol Hotel, located between the Bolshoi Theatre and the Kremlin's Red Square. Entering the front doors of the Metropol was a step into a swirling island of internationalism in a sea of urban decay and reconstruction, where even the bellhops spoke perfect English. The newly refurbished grand hotel was at the site of the first riots of the Communist Revolution against the Czar. It was obviously now the headquarters of the Capitalist Revolution overthrowing the Communists.

I had the rest of the waning day to myself as my World Bank people were occupied with meetings. I decided to go exploring, even though I was somewhat on edge with reports I'd heard in the States of the rampant crime in Moscow and a country boy's unease at just being in a city environment. Because I was at a total loss with the language and unintelligible script on street signs, I made small, cautious half-block forays in all directions from the hotel, getting braver with each turn. I saw all manner of wondrous and unexpected things, and each time I returned to the hotel unmugged and, as yet, unarrested by the KGB. On my fourth trip, now three blocks from the hotel, I stood face to face with St. Basil's Cathedral in Red Square, the cultural icon known the world over. I was overcome by emotion seeing firsthand this astounding work of art. For the remainder of the daylight hours, I continued exploring my new environment, coming back to St. Basil's time and time again to view this wondrous creation from yet another angle.

The next evening my World Bank companions and I boarded the night train to Nizhny Novgorod, Russia's third-largest city and the headquarters of Russia's land reform experiment. Nizhny is formerly the city of Gorki, taking back its old name after the collapse of the Soviet regime. Until the 1992 name change, Nizhny had been a closed city, allowing no Western visitors or communications. It was a place where dissidents were sent to get them out of circulation and, by Western accounts, a prison city within a prison society. Those times behind us, in 1994 Nizhny Novgorod was one of the most progressive cities in all of Russia, in the vanguard of all types of social, legal, and economic reforms.

The dashing young Russia editor of *The Economist,* the British magazine, just happened to be on our train. I shared a table in the dining car with him and the World Bank Russia Land Reform project head, a gorgeous Harvard-educated young woman. As the train rolled steadily toward our destination, we consumed some strange stew and the only other thing on the menu: that Russian staple, straight shots of vodka. After two hours of this I was reeling. In addition, I hadn't really slept since I'd left the Breaks Ranch a couple of days, half a world and twelve time zones away.

When I returned to my sleeping compartment and got into bed, I was expecting blessed rest to finally overtake me. But as the train rumbled on into the vast Russian night, there were sounds coming through the paper-thin walls from the neighboring compartment in the international language of primal love.

When my fellow travelers finally quieted, I could no longer think of sleep. The rest of the night I found myself springing to the window each time a new light appeared in the blackness, not wanting to miss anything, and not knowing what would come next.

The Illustrators

• • • • • • • • • • • • • • • • • • •

Vern Groff has been one of the Northwest's leading graphic designers for over twenty years. He is the owner of Studio Group in Portland, Oregon. Vern's images, Plow the Back Forty on Your Kitchen Table, Zen Ranching, and *The Farming Game* logo were created in collaboration with the author. Visit *The Farming Game* web site to see Celilo Falls on the Columbia another image this partnership has produced.

Blake Rohrbacher left the Breaks Ranch at sixteen to attend Yale University where he rowed on the heavyweight crew and created a cartoon strip for the student weekly. He currently works in New York doing computer graphics and dreams of graduate school. Blake drew the images for the text.

To order the cardboard classic or the computer version for Windows®:

The Weekend Farmer Company
P.O. Box 896
Goldendale, Washington 98620

Fax: 509-773-6464

Phone: 1-800-222-GAME

Visit our web site: www.farmgame.com

To order additional copies of

Zen Ranching

and

The Farming Game

Book: $14.95 • Shipping/Handling: $3.50

BookPartners, Inc.
P.O. Box 922
Wilsonville, Oregon 97070

Fax: 503-682-8684

Phone: 1-800-895-7323